Counselling and Helping Carers

J. Mitchell Noon

Communication and Counselling in Health Care Series
Series editor: Hilton Davis

Counselling and Helping Carers

J. Mitchell Noon

*Consultant Clinical Psychologist
at Cornwall Healthcare Trust, Truro, UK*

Medical advisor: Alastair Macdonald

*Lewisham and Guy's Mental Health Trust,
Lewisham Hospital, London, UK*

 Published by The British Psychological Society

First published in 1999 by BPS Books (The British Psychological Society), St Andrews House, 48 Princess Road East, Leicester LE1 7DR, UK.

Distributed exclusively in North America by Paul H. Brookes Publishing Co., Inc., PO Box 10624, Baltimore, Maryland 21285, USA.

A catalogue record for this book is available from the British Library.

ISBN 1 85433 272 4

Typeset by Ralph J. Footring, Derby

Printed by Antony Rowe Limited, Reading, Berks.

OTHER TITLES IN THE SERIES:
Counselling Parents of Children with Chronic Illness or Disability by Hilton Davis
Counselling for Heart Disease by Paul Bennett
Counselling in Obstetrics and Gynaecology by Myra Hunter
Counselling People with Diabetes by Richard Shillitoe
Counselling in Terminal Care and Bereavement by Colin Murray Parkes, Marilyn Relf and Ann Couldrick
Counselling People with Disfigurement by Eileen Bradbury
Counselling Children with Chronic Medical Conditions by Melinda Edwards and Hilton Davis

Dedication

For Angie, Tom and Jo.

Acknowledgements

I am grateful to Hilton Davis for his editorial support, guidance and exceptional patience.

With particular thanks to 'Pom'.

Contents

List of Tables

List of Figures

Foreword

What do carers want? A brief look at the Web page of Carers National UK will give you a good idea – financial support from improved benefits, more efficient support from primary health care teams and social services, more understanding employers, and breaks from caring. Top of the list is 'Acknowledgement' – but in the shape of an Act of Parliament that gives carers legal rights. Conspicuous by its absence in this list is any mention of the sort of psychological and emotional help that this book is all about. Here is a puzzle for those of us, sometimes carers and ex-carers ourselves, whose work necessarily brings us into contact with carers in distress. Psychologists, psychiatrists, mental health nurses, occupational therapists, social workers and others constantly encounter carers who clearly need exactly the careful and thoughtful approach taken by Mitchell Noon in this book. Although it may be mentioned by carers in their literature, why do they themselves not give much more prominence to the need for emotional and psychological help?

There are several possible answers. There is the fear that asking for this support will somehow invalidate demands for practical and financial help, that all that will be provided is some barely trained and ill-managed 'counsellor' who will listen endlessly or advise intrusively while lack of money, time and practical aids overwhelm the carer. There is the possibility that carers deliberately suppress the emotional and psychological sides of themselves in order to carry on caring. Perhaps they feel that once the floodgates are opened they will not be able to fulfil their duty by carrying on. It is also possible that in the caring role is an implicit rejection of being cared for. To my knowledge no one has systematically investigated these factors, so they remain speculative.

Another explanation lies in epidemiology. Carers National UK estimates that there are seven million carers in the UK, and it could be that the majority do not feel the need for emotional support because it is satisfied – by family, friends, and 'front-line' professionals like general practitioners. Specialists only see a small fraction of all carers – the exceptional cases, in whom these normal support systems have, almost by definition, failed. According to this argument the vast majority of carers need no particular emotional and psychological help from outside their normal relationships.

There is, however, evidence that this argument is untenable. Surveys of carers have consistently shown that a significant proportion have frank emotional disorders, and that the severity of these disorders is at least as great as that seen by specialists like psychologists and psychiatrists in their patients. A particular problem is depressive disorder, sometimes of a severity that requires medication as well as psychological help – the carer can be so low as not to be able to make use of the latter until a 'vicious circle' of chemical imbalance in the brain has been restored by a course of medication. This state can be missed when those helping the carer attribute all the carer's difficulties to the stress of caring. It is almost as if they say to a carer who is not sleeping or eating well, losing weight, constantly gloomy, anxious or tearful, 'How do you expect to feel any different, looking after someone with advanced dementia?' Although the proportion of carers in this sort of severe state is fortunately not high, it is crucial that they are recognized and treated early.

At the risk of pedantry, I conclude with the use of the word 'need'. A friend of mine once endured a long, hot drive with one of his small children, aged about six, constantly demanding an ice-cream. 'I need an ice-cream!' came the cry, piercing and endlessly repeated. What did he mean? 'I want an ice-cream!' had long been abandoned as failing to achieve the desired end. There have been many attempts to define 'need', few totally satisfactory. My own favourite is, bizarrely, the Department of Health's – a need for something is defined as the ability to benefit from it. Mitchell Noon's careful and clearly thought-out book brings excellent advice to those who try to help carers of all sorts, caring for people with all sorts of problems, and I have no doubt that everyone who comes into contact with carers *needs* to read it.

Alastair Macdonald
Professor of Old Age Psychiatry
Guy's, King's and St Thomas' Schools of Medicine,
Dentistry and Biomedical Sciences
King's College, London

Preface to the Series

People who suffer chronic disease or disability are confronted by problems that are as much psychological as physical, and involve all members of their family and the wider social network. Psychosocial adaptation is important in its own right, in terms of making necessary changes in lifestyle, altering aspirations or coping with an uncertain future. However, it may also influence the effectiveness of the diagnostic and treatment processes, and hence eventual outcomes.

As a consequence, healthcare, whether preventive or treatment-oriented, must encompass the psychosocial integrated with the physical, at all phases of the life cycle and at all stages of disease. The basis of this is skilled communication and counselling by all involved in providing services, professionally or voluntarily. Everyone, from the student to the experienced practitioner, can benefit from appropriate training in this area, where the social skills required are complex and uncertain.

Although there is a sizeable research literature related to counselling and communication in the area of healthcare, specialist texts for training purposes are scarce. The current series was, therefore, conceived as a practical resource for all who work in health services. Each book is concerned with a specific area of healthcare. The authors have been asked to provide detailed information, from the patient's perspective, about the problems (physical, psychological and social) faced by patients and their families. Each book examines the role of counselling and communication in the process of helping people to come to terms and deal with these problems, and presents usable frameworks as a guide to the helping process. Detailed and practical descriptions of the major qualities, abilities and skills that are required to provide the most effective help for patients are included.

The intention is to stimulate professional and voluntary helpers alike to explore their efforts at supportive communication. It is hoped that by so doing, they become sufficiently aware of patient difficulties and the processes of adaptation, and more able to facilitate positive adjustment. The aims of the series will have been met if patients and families feel someone has listened and if they feel respected in their struggle for health. A central theme is the effort to make people feel better about themselves and able to face the future, no matter how bleak, with dignity.

Hilton Davis
Series Editor

1

Introduction

Terminology

The terminology used throughout this book makes the following important distinctions:

- The term *carer* refers to the individual who has day-to-day responsibility for looking after a person who is ill or disabled and unable to live independently. Most often the carer will be a relative or the partner of the person cared for.
- The term *person cared for* refers to the recipient of care.
- The term *helper* describes a range of professional people, including health-care staff – nurses, doctors, professions allied to medicine (physiotherapists, occupational therapists, speech therapists, radiographers, dieticians) as well as others, such as social workers, care assistants and workers in non-statutory organizations. They deal with the specific needs of patients or clients on an everyday basis and they may also frequently encounter carers, as a by-product of their involvement with patients and clients.

The needs of carers are sometimes unclear and many helpers are uncertain about their role in relation to carers and how to respond to their needs as they become apparent. All of these helpers will use basic helping skills in their everyday work. They may wish, therefore, to develop these basic skills in relation to the specific needs of carers. This book is written for professional helpers and is designed to enhance their basic helping skills. The book will also be of relevance to volunteers in established organizations whose work brings them into contact with clients and their carers.

The helping skills I will be describing in this book are usually termed *counselling skills*. These are the foundations of effective helping. They are to be distinguished from *formal counselling*, which is a specific activity undertaken by trained counsellors.

Counselling skills are, of course, the basis of formal counselling, but the use of counselling skills is not restricted to formal counselling. I hope to be able to show that these skills are fundamental to all helping relationships and not just formal counselling *per se*. In order to avoid any potential confusion between formal counselling and counselling skills, I will use the term *helping skills* to describe the latter.

Organization of the Book

The book is organized in the following way. In this chapter a specific case is described in some detail. The aim of this is to give as vivid a picture as possible of the experience of one carer which I believe will be familiar to many carers and helpers. You will very likely recognize some of the issues identified, and you will find them developed and extended in other case studies throughout the book.

Chapter 2 sets the scene by providing basic information about the extent of the caring role within the population as a whole and describes a variety of characteristics of caring which contribute to the special demands of the task and the difficulties that can be faced by carers. These characteristics of caring are related to conventions and norms, within society and between ethnic and cultural sub-groups, about what constitutes adequate or inadequate care. This is the basis on which carers judge their own standards of care and whether or not they have coped with their responsibilities.

Chapter 3 develops the theme of the carer's experience in more detail. A model of coping is presented. The aim here is to provide the reader with a look behind the scenes, so to speak. It is a view of the processes underlying behaviour and is intended to extend the helper's knowledge about the relationship between what happens in the carer's daily life and the impact of those events on the carer as a person: on his or her sense of self-worth. On the basis of this relationship it may become clearer why certain difficulties in coping arise in particular instances.

In Chapter 4 the specific needs of carers are identified in more detail. It is argued that carers can be distinguished from other populations who may seek help but are not engaged in the task of caring. These differences have important implications for the provision of help. Carers have a variety of different needs which can be met in different ways. There is further discussion of the ethnic and cultural factors that influence coping, help-seeking and help-giving.

In Chapter 5 the basic skills of helping are introduced. The chapter begins by stressing the importance of the helping relationship and the conditions whereby this can be fostered. Specific guidance is then given about the details of each component skill in the helping process. A variety of case examples are interspersed throughout the chapter to illustrate the points made.

In Chapter 6 the helping skills described in the previous chapter are related to specific strategies for helping. Three broad and overlapping strategies are discussed:

1. advice and information;
2. support and emotional help;
3. problem-solving.

Numerous case examples are provided to illustrate the points made. There is also a discussion of more complex issues which introduces the question of the limits of certain types of help and when the need for specialist help may arise.

Finally, in Chapter 7 the focus is switched to the helper. Issues associated with the helping role are identified and discussed and some ideas are provided about how to deal with these issues. Evidence is reviewed of the effectiveness of the skills described in this book and there is a discussion about how the benefits of helping may best be identified and evaluated.

Mrs A: A Life in Ten Paragraphs

The following extract is a more or less verbatim account given by a carer I saw as a patient early in my clinical career. My meetings with her made a lasting impression on me, not least because of the clarity with which she expressed her feelings of loss. I still have a letter she sent after our meetings had finished in which she recorded her experience of the impact of her husband's illness and I reproduce it here, with some amendments to preserve confidentiality and with thanks for the insights she gave me.

In subsequent years this experience has been confirmed, in one way or another, by many other carers I have seen professionally.

The loss is great, the anguish can be severe and the adjustment is always immensely difficult. With any loss, though, it is possible to find ways of working through the experience and, ultimately, of coping. This book is dedicated to that aim.

How can I describe my feelings about a life together – a partnership for all those years – set fair at my husband's retirement in 1978, with plans for doing the sorts of things we had always enjoyed; with a modest income that would allow us to carry out our plans – now completely destroyed.

We'd planned retirement carefully. We weren't rich by any means, but we'd have enough to gain some enjoyment and some rewards after a lifetime of work. We would travel. We'd always loved that. And we would continue a relationship that had always been so close and affectionate. We were real friends, even after all this time. And now ... now all that is gone.

I think back to the good times. 1978 was such a good year. We had friends living in Italy. We'd known them years and they were close friends. We spent three months in Italy with them. We were guests at a wedding just outside Naples. We spent a week at a vineyard near Florence helping bring in the grapes and then feasting and drinking in the wonderful evenings. I remember we talked about politics and justice, all the things that had passionately interested me and John all our lives. We drove to Rimini and swam and sunbathed. We saw parts of the country that few tourists ever see. It felt like life was just beginning.

In 1979 we went on a trip to Southern Ireland, driving all around the remote beautiful country. Looking back I can see now that things were never the same again. In May 1979 my husband suffered an attack that was never properly identified and in 1980 he underwent four operations in six months. From then on he became a pale shadow of his former self.

In August 1982 it was clear that my husband was not keeping his habitual, meticulous accounts, and this showed considerable deterioration. From then on it seemed nothing could be done and we struggled on trying to cope with the tremendous changes taking place that turned a loving, humorous companion of nearly 50 years into a querulous, depressed person. We visited our friends in Italy again in 1982 and 1983 in search of sun and sea and to try to recapture that spirit of 1978, but the tremendous enjoyment and excitement of the earlier visit was gone. The spirit, the wit, the intelligence that made 'him' had vanished.

By February 1984 he was very much worse. Parkinson's disease was diagnosed. Our doctor said he had never seen him look so poorly. His health and personality deteriorated rapidly. Tests carried out in May 1984 confirmed the diagnosis and in July a minor heart attack further impaired his mobility and speech, which did not respond to physio- and speech therapy. A brain scan in August 1984 showed brain damage and no prospect of improvement. I realized that my efforts to find treatment for him were not going to be successful and since September 1984 I have been trying to cope with the problem of a beloved partner, a much loved companion and friend, husband, lover, who now cannot understand what is happening and can take no further part in what has been a loving, caring, satisfying relationship of 50 years.

In 35 years in public service I have come across many people who even in the fullness of youth were not able to communicate either in writing or verbally; but my husband was always a communicator. He could always defuse a situation with wit and humour. We shared thoughts, interests and plans and lived a full and happy life. I have tried to lift him out of his despair and depression and stimulate his interest; to cope with his suicidal fits of frustration, but the worst of all is the mental confusion inherent in his condition: diabetes, Parkinson's disease, a heart attack, and Alzheimer's disease. When I look back on our life together and all our plans I realise they were so many pipe dreams. He doesn't remember where we have been, or when, or why. Photographs collected over many years are just pictures, not memories. Our past happiness is non-existent for him. For me it is a bitter-sweet memory that makes the present seem so much worse.

In my arrogance or conceit I wrote in March 1985 that I would cope; that my earlier feeling that I would go mad was not likely; that though it would be a totally different life from that we had planned I would be able to look after him. Now even that belief has been taken from me. I suffered an ischaemic spasm that left me with a mouth awry and impaired speech for some hours. This shocked and frightened me into the realization that I am not invincible and might not be able to cope. A few hours without articulate speech showed me that there could be situations outside my control entirely and about which I would be helpless – and my husband not even able to use a telephone. I had come to accept his helplessness, now I had to realize that I too could be vulnerable. The condition was minor in terms of severity and may not recur, or only infrequently, but it is a warning. It could tip over into something more serious if I continue trying to care for my husband at home. Now I can visit him, but if I had continued as I was I may not even have been able to do that.

My husband alternates between crying and depression when he is aware of what has happened and complete oblivion when he is not aware. When he is like this he doesn't recognize his surroundings, nor even the identities of friends and family. I have visited him every day until recently and I still find it heart-rending seeing him now compared with how he was.

I have to record the loving husband I have lost. Our grand-children will need to know Grandpa as he was, as I have known him, so I must set out the man as he was, as I knew and loved him for 50 years. It's so hard to say this, but the man I see now isn't the same person. It's the same body, but the person no longer exists. I will always do my best for him as he is, but I realize now that John is dead.

> *'While still I may, I write for you*
> *The love I lived, the life I knew'*

Issues Raised

The above extract is an eloquent description of the difficulties faced by a carer and a testimony to the capacity to survive and, ultimately, cope. The issues raised are common to many carers.

As I re-read the account, I am struck by a number of themes that emerge. There is the painful contrast between past and present. There are memories of an earlier fulfilling life. There are plans, dreams and expectations of a future together, sharing the fruits of earlier efforts. In other words, there was a time when life was predictable, had a direction and a sense of control. This contrasts with the sense of disintegration as those earlier plans dissolve before the carer's eyes. There is a gradual and increasing feeling within the carer of impending doom as her husband's condition worsens. Plans for the future are replaced by memories of the past. One can see the development of a sense of unfairness and despair. There is the pain of contrast between the fruitful past and the barren present.

Then there are the early attempts by the carer to cope: what may be termed the 'heroic phase'. Eventually, the struggle exerts a toll and she herself becomes ill. She begins to question her own sanity: a real sign of losing control. She feels she is fading.

Paradoxically, though, alongside the personal crisis there also emerges a realization by the carer that she must begin to look after herself if there is to be any future for either herself or her husband. This may appear obvious to the outsider, looking in. Of course, we may comment, she has to look after herself if she is going to cope with the demands of her task. But from the carer's perspective it may not be at all obvious. Her view of the world has for a long time consisted only of one perceived need: that of her husband. To question this seems at first virtually heretical. That is why it had to get to the point where she was forced by her ill health to acknowledge this need. Yet when it is acknowledged we begin to see the foundations of coping taking shape as the carer recognizes the reality of her situation.

Interspersed with all of these developments there is the frequent recognition that her husband is not the same person he once was: he cannot be, nor ever will. This is immensely painful. At first it feels like betrayal. Later it becomes an acknowledgement of an inescapable reality.

Gradually she becomes reconciled to her circumstances. She recognizes the need both to cope with the material difficulties of caring while also recording, for her family, her memories of the relationship that is now past. This gives a new meaning to her experiences and with it she develops the ability to move forwards into the future.

Aims of the Book

The principal aim of this book is to enable helpers to be more effective in addressing the needs of carers: to recognize and respond to the carer's difficult task of negotiating the complex path from crisis to coping. In order to achieve this we will consider the ways in which carers experience the task of caring: how illness in someone close has an effect not just on the ill individual, but also on the *relationship* between that individual and significant others. Caring for another brings new dimensions to relationships. It stretches the bounds of existing assumptions. It challenges cherished beliefs about the relationship between you and your partner, child, parent or relative. Ultimately, it challenges your self-concept. The foundations of your own self – your very being – are shaken and, perhaps, upturned.

The role of parent, or partner, or caring relative develops over time. For example, a parent may strive to be the provider for and protector of his or her child. But with the child's serious illness there arises a powerful threat to that role. A sense of powerlessness and failure may develop. What happens to those emotions? Are they acknowledged and expressed? If so, how and in what form? If not, why not? Or, to take another example, a marriage has for years been a partnership: despite its ups and downs it has, on balance, been a reciprocal relationship between two mutually respectful and caring individuals. Then one becomes seriously ill and the relationship is changed. It is natural for the focus of concern to be upon the person who is ill. But what about the supposedly healthy survivor? How often is there recognition of the full extent of the impact of the other's illness on the partner? The reciprocity and the mutuality of the prior relationship have been undermined. The partner has been deprived; something has been wrenched away. The balance has been changed. What sense does the partner, now the carer, make of this? How does the changed relationship between the couple develop from here?

Of course, not all parents find it easy to love their children and not all partners live in mutual and satisfying relationships. But in these circumstances too the effects of serious illness can be profound. Skewed past relationships provide fertile ground for issues of guilt, anger, retribution and shame when those relationships are changed.

The aims of this book, then, are twofold: first of all, to examine the experiences of carers; secondly, to consider how help may best be provided by those who are involved in a professional helping role. This will entail:

- illustrating the effects on carers of the role of caring – the ways in which caring exerts psychological and material pressures on carers and how these affect thoughts, feelings and behaviour;
- encouraging professional helpers to provide optimal help – to recognize and respond to the distress of carers and to help carers to come to terms both with the effects of caring and with the task of future care;
- enabling helpers to be aware of different types of helping and to recognize more fully what kind of help may be necessary, when and for whom;

- considering the special characteristics of carers as a population compared with others who are not engaged in the task of caring but who may seek help.

Throughout the book there will be a number of illustrations of the points made, in the form of examples based on actual cases, although details will be changed in order to preserve confidentiality. The case examples are drawn from my own experience as a clinical psychologist. Some are carers I have seen myself, because their difficulties were interfering with their lives and they had sought formal psychological help. Others are carers I have heard about, in my dealings with other health-care staff, social services staff and volunteers. However, while I believe the examples of carers' experiences provided in this book are reasonably broad, I am conscious of the fact that they can only ever be partial. Professionals working in different environments will encounter other kinds of problems among the carers with whom they are involved.

I am also aware of the danger of overemphasizing the difficulties encountered by carers. It is not my intention to suggest that all carers experience problems all of the time. Many carers clearly gain pleasure and fulfilment in caring and cope well with their task. Nevertheless, this book, by its nature, is intended for those occasions when difficulties occur; and for most carers, some of the problems described in this book are likely to occur some of the time.

Despite these reservations I hope that the themes and issues described herein will be of general relevance and will be recognizable to professional helpers whose work brings them into contact with carers.

2

The Task of Caring

Much is written about the experience of people who are ill: patients directly affected by disease or disability. But relatively little is said about the emotional and material effects of illness on others who are close to the patient: friends, relatives or close family. Yet the effects of illness may be no less profound for those others. Each individual in the intricate network of relationships is touched in some way by the changes wreaked by illness or disability. The focus of this book is on those others, and in particular on that specific other who takes on the role of *informal carer*; the person charged with the task of providing unpaid, informal care, on a regular and often daily basis, for a large proportion of his or her time. The relationship between the carer and the person cared for is varied. For instance, the carer may be the parent of a chronically ill child, the son or daughter of a parent with a disabling illness, the partner of a person with chronic illness or injury, or the relative of someone involved in a serious and disabling accident. I will provide a variety of relevant examples of these relationships in the text.

The Size of the Task

In all societies carers constitute a significant proportion of the population. In the UK it is estimated that there are about 5.7 million carers nationally (which is 13% of adults over 16 years) – 3.3 million women, 2.4 million men (Rowlands, 1998). Of these, 1.9 million are caring for someone in the same home, 1.7 million spend at least 20 hours a week as carers and 3.7 million are the main source of care for a dependent other (*ibid.*). These figures have been fairly stable over the last ten years in the UK (see Green, 1988). There is no reason to doubt that comparable statistics are likely to be found in other parts of the world, and that in all societies carers are a substantial part of the general population. Their task is onerous and without them existing statutory services would be unable to cope. It must be acknowledged that carers are a major source of support not just for those for whom they care, but also for the formal health and social services within society. Without carers, these services would be overwhelmed. Clearly, carers deserve to be treated with respect.

Governments acknowledge the essential role played by informal carers – 'the great bulk of community care is provided by family, friends and neighbours' (Department of Health, 1993) – and there is recognition that statutory services have a duty to identify and provide for the needs of carers. As a result, in some countries specific proposals have been made about ways in which the material needs of carers might be met. There is also a growing recognition of the emotional impact of caring. However, despite this, little formal guidance exists on the provision of emotional help. Indeed, there is some evidence that the provision of emotional help for carers may be more complex than anticipated. Carers have particular needs and face unique demands which distinguish them as a group from others coping with stressful circumstances. An understanding of the nature of carers' material and emotional needs and the specific characteristics of the distress experienced by them will enable professional helpers to respond appropriately to those needs.

Characteristics of Caring

In the following chapters I will present specific details about the characteristics of carers and the needs associated with their task. There will be a description of the process of coping: why do people cope or fail to cope? The answers to this question will provide a framework around which the difficulties of caring can be understood. There will also be some examples of the social and cultural influences that determine a carer's attitude and approach to caring. As I have said, the aim is to enable professional *helpers* who come into contact with carers to be more effective in the help they offer. Accordingly, having identified carers' needs, I will describe the foundation skills of helping and how these may be developed for that purpose.

As a preliminary to all of this, I would first like to provide an informal description of some general characteristics of caring, derived from my own experience of working with carers over a number of years. The particular difficulties associated with being a carer compared with other forms of stressful experience derive to a large extent from the *indirect* nature of the task. This underpins a variety of features of caring which contribute to the special characteristics of the task. It will be helpful, in considering these, to relate them to a specific example: the case of Sarah.

Case example: 'What is wrong with me?'

Sarah, in her fifties, had been married for three years. It was her second marriage and Alan, her present husband, was several years older than her. Sadly, just 12 months after their marriage, Alan had suffered a serious illness and become severely disabled. As a result, Sarah became his carer. She did not flinch from her responsibilities, but adopted the task of caring as a natural extension of her prior relationship with her husband. Alan needed help with everything: washing, dressing, going to the toilet, eating, drinking: he was entirely dependent on Sarah. Despite coping admirably in many ways with Alan's needs, in time she found herself becoming more and more irritated with him. She shocked herself one day by shouting at him so angrily that she felt ashamed. 'I just exploded,' she said. Afterwards she was full of remorse. She asked herself, what had he done to deserve that? How could she be so awful and hurtful to Alan? He could not help being the way he is. He could not answer back.

She began to perceive herself as an 'awful woman'. She recalled all the occasions she had been irritated in the past. 'How dreadful,' she thought, 'There must be something wrong with me.' Her behaviour had contradicted all her beliefs about what is right and how one person should behave towards another in need. It was only as a result of a chance conversation with the district nurse that she discovered that carers often feel frustrated and irritated and at the end of their tether. It was not just her. The district nurse, in her comments, had normalized *the experience for Sarah. This provided a context within which Sarah could see her behaviour as understandable, even to be expected.*

Many carers feel like this, but not all carers know that it is a common experience. The lack of this context can engender feelings of guilt and self-deprecation leading to a downwards spiral of difficulties in coping.

Sarah's experience is typical. Her self-neglect, her frustrations, her sense of isolation, her self-deprecation can all be found in one guise or another in the experience of many carers. The consequences of these experiences are various. In some cases, they may represent a transient disruption in the process of caring which can be placed into perspective by the simple comment of another person, such as the nurse. In other cases, they may continue unchecked and develop into more serious problems both for the carer and the person cared for. A knowledge of these characteristics, therefore, will enable potential helpers to identify difficulties early in the process and, by offering help, pre-empt the development of more serious problems.

Characteristic 1: whose problem is it anyway?

This refers to the *indirect* nature of the causes of a carer's problems. 'Why am I upset? He is the one who is ill. I'm the lucky one; the survivor. How can I complain?' These are very typical comments made by carers and underpin the frustration experienced by Sarah. The central issue is the *perceived illegitimacy* of the distress experienced by the carer in relation to the problems of the person cared for. This, in turn, is associated with guilt and shame. But it is important to acknowledge that the carer's distress *is* legitimate. It is impossible not to be challenged as an individual by the demands of caring; and it must not be considered surprising if the carer shows signs and symptoms of the strain of the task in the form of occasional frustration, anger or despair.

Characteristic 2: saint or sinner?

The perfect carer is selfless, dedicated, tireless, uncomplaining. As compassionate as Mother Theresa; as relentless as Joan of Arc in pursuing the cause of the loved one and, perhaps, as liable to martyrdom. The good news, however, is that 100% of carers I have known fail to meet these criteria. Nevertheless, we really must not underestimate the pressure exerted by social stereotypes of caring and by the failure to live up to impossible ideals and expectations. In addition, there is a real issue of self-denial in terms of the carer's needs, which are often deferred, ignored or relegated in the face of the task of caring. Looking at the example of Sarah, her irritation had been founded upon self-denial. She had spent so much time thinking about someone else that she had neglected her own needs. However, neglected needs have a habit of surfacing in the guise of resentment, irritation and anger.

Characteristic 3: no choice, no control!

Many people do have clear ethical or religious standards that guide their actions. However, while some are born carers and some achieve the capacity to care, many have caring thrust upon them. Even if an individual's aspirations are realistic, the transition from 'ordinary human being' to carer is prone to difficulties and these difficulties need to be seen as normal, understandable and indeed inevitable, rather than a sign of failure.

The problem with being cast into an unchosen role is that the carer may feel that as well as no choice there is no control. If there appears to be no control over events, the carer may begin to feel frustrated or defeated by the task. Once again, the seeds of anger or depression are sown. In either case, the experience of being out of control is demoralizing. Demoralized carers will tend to care less well and become more self-critical as a consequence. As their care deteriorates, so they enter into a vicious circle of self-fulfilling prophesy.

Characteristic 4: vicarious pain

I think it is generally true to say that it is easier to adjust to your own illness or disability than it is to adjust to the pain of another for whom you care. Certainly I have known carers who find this to be the case. Perhaps the clearest example is to be found in the parents of children who are ill. The natural wish to protect is denied by an uncontrollable illness or disability. Thus the carer is afflicted both by the visible distress of the other as well as by personal distress born of a desire to protect rendered impotent by events. This impotence may lead to feelings of failure and depression, on the one hand, or seemingly in-explicable anger, on the other.

Characteristic 5: relative values

The relationship between wife and husband as partners is different to that between one as carer for the other. A man or woman caring for his or her parent creates a new dynamic in the relationship. A parent caring for an ill or injured child has a different relationship to a parent caring for a healthy child. All of these differences are largely created by circumstances that are unchosen and unwelcome. Marital and parental relationships inside the family and social relationships outside the family are all potentially changed. Priorities are revised, either deliberately or as an unplanned consequence of providing care.

Adjusting to these changes is difficult at best and can sometimes lead to serious disharmony and jeopardize relationships within the social and family nexus. It is not unusual for carers, friends and family to feel a sense of failure as a consequence and, of course, anger and resentment towards the person cared for are not uncommon, but are often unspoken.

Characteristic 6: a provisional existence

Frankl (1959) describes a number of examples of people living an existence without a clear future and without an obvious goal. He terms this a 'provisional existence': 'With the end of uncertainty there came the uncertainty of the end. It was impossible to foresee whether or when, if at all, this form of existence would end' (p. 111).

Carers too experience such uncertainties. The future is an unknown quantity. How long will their task last? Can they cope physically, mentally? Are there any personal goals left or are all goals other-directed? Certainly there is an immense and sometimes shocking difference between life as it was before the task of caring and life as it is now that caring is the priority and this, of course, requires considerable adjustment. I have known one kind, compassionate, caring individual describe her existence as a 'life sentence'.

Conventions and Norms: Models of Care

The characteristics described above have in common the fact that carers bring to their task a basic set of beliefs and assumptions about what is involved in caring: what is *appropriate*, what is *normal*, what is *good care* and *poor care*. These basic beliefs are derived from standards learnt from family and from society at large. The set of beliefs that you or I have about what is appropriate behaviour in a particular context contributes to the internal models that underpin our behaviour, in this case the act of providing care, and it is useful, in understanding the individual's response to the task of caring, to be aware of the existence of these internal models.

As a general guide, there are a number of examples of what might be called *relationship models* that are transmitted within a society by the rules of convention. These include a *parental* model, a *partner* model and an *offspring* model, referring to the relationships that convention determines individuals *ought to have* within the family or partnership. In turn, each of these models has a number of forms that reflect cultural and sub-cultural norms and expectations (ethnicity, religion, class, gender, sexual preference) within particular groups in society. Thus, for instance, there is no one correct model of parenting: a range of possibilities exists. Similarly there is no single partner model and no unique relationship between adult offspring and their parents. Nevertheless, for all their variability, it is apparent that there are also notable commonalities and people do hold a set of conventional beliefs about the nature of relationships which they carry with them into the task of caring (see Hall, 1990). If there can be said to be a carer model, then it is some amalgam of these other relationship models. The task for the carer is to find a set of operating assumptions about the relationship between himself or herself and the person cared for. The question is how successfully this carer model is adapted and adopted by each individual carer.

Bearing this in mind it is inevitable that the carer will begin the task of caring on the basis of assumptions about the appropriate relationship between himself or herself and the person cared for: a model of what *ought to be*. In addition, whether the carer is the parent or partner or offspring of the person cared for, the newly established caring relationship will replace or supplement an existing relationship. Sometimes this change of relationship is itself the main problem experienced by carers and those cared for. Take the example of a carer who has to take responsibility for toileting the partner. It is likely that the only experience of toileting another will be in relation to a child. Thus, in that particular act of caring, the partner model has to be extended to incorporate a task that is usually associated with the parental model. It will be apparent that this can be a source of distress both to the carer and, of course, to the person cared for. In this case the extent to which the transition between partner role and parental role is coped with will affect the quality of care given and received.

For the *helper* who may be involved with the carer, the difficult task is to be sensitive to the balance between these various models as they are adopted within a particular caring relationship. As a generalization, the key word is *balance*. Problems usually become apparent when one model dominates to the exclusion of others. For instance, a formerly parental relationship between a parent and young child may become reversed as the parent falls ill. The child then takes on a parental role within the family at a time when his or her own parenting is incomplete. The child may also become responsible for younger siblings, or may have the burden of housework or cooking at a time when other children have the freedom to play and study and form social relationships with their peers. In effect, the child is forced to relinquish his or her childhood. It is often only in adulthood that the full impact of that deprivation becomes fully apparent. The child has suffered a great loss in the form of impoverished parenting and also in the development of the social skills of relating to others of the same age.

Another example is to be seen in the relationship between partners when one becomes the carer of the other. If, as in the example of toileting, there is a need for the previous relationship to incorporate new tasks, such as looking after the other's bodily requirements – toileting, bathing, feeding – then the question is how this affects that relationship. Sometimes the partner copes with the new parental expectations of caring by abandoning the partner model altogether and adopting the parental model full time. The change from the implicit *mutuality* of a partner relationship to the *dependency* of a parental relationship can have an adverse effect for both the carer and the person cared for.

In addition to incorporating new tasks into the relationship between carer and person cared for, there is the problem of relinquishing old roles and expectations. A carer may have to relinquish social and/or sexual activities with the person cared for when these were formerly part of that relationship. The adult offspring of an elderly parent may feel caught between responsibilities to the parent and to his or her own partner and children.

The problems described represent dilemmas faced by carers. Once again, *balance* is central: how can the carer achieve a balance between responsibilities to others (person cared for, own family, friends) and responsibilities to self? With our models of *how* we should act come the baselines against which we judge ourselves. Thus *self-appraisal* is undertaken in relation to the models of behaviour adopted, in this case the models of care. Self-appraisal raises the question: 'How well am I doing my task?' The answer may be broadly positive or negative and if it is the latter we have the foundation for self-deprecation and all of its ramifications which lead, ultimately, to failing to cope. In Chapter 3 we will examine more closely the relationship between behaviour and self-appraisal.

Race, ethnicity and culture

One particular and potent influence on the model of care adopted by any carer is the cultural background of that carer. Most societies are multi-racial, multi-ethnic and multi-cultural. Helpers must be aware of the influence of this variability and be able to react with sensitivity to the issues raised. There are, of course, a multitude of different groups within any given society and it is impossible to refer to all of them. In this book, therefore, I will focus in this and the following chapters on just a few examples. However, the points made do have a wider relevance and can be applied to other groups.

Let us begin with definitions. The term *race* is used to refer to biological differences between groups, although this is considered a scientifically unsound basis for categorizing human groups (Littlefield *et al.*, 1982) and is preserved as a category because of its social rather than scientific basis. *Ethnicity* is self-identity derived from previous generations with whom the individual associates himself or herself (Thomas, 1986). People from the same ethnic group may, nevertheless, subscribe to different cultural systems and people from different ethnic groups may share the same cultural system. *Culture* is learnt. It is the shared system of symbols and meanings within the larger society and incorporates a variety of social conventions, values and norms.

A person from one ethnic group may have a shared ethnic background with his or her parents and grandparents, but may subscribe to a different culture. Perhaps the clearest example of this is the case of second- or third-generation immigrants. Their parents and grandparents may have retained the culture of the society from which they emigrated, while they themselves have adopted the norms and conventions of the new society. Typical examples can be found in South Asian immigrants in Britain, or British immigrants in Australia or New Zealand, or Latin American immigrants in the United States. In all cases, the developing generations retain something of the values and beliefs of their old society, while at the same time acquiring values and beliefs from their new society. This can, of course, lead to conflict, both internally, within the person, and externally, between generations, and the task of adapting to these various influences is itself a cause of much stress.

In the case of caring for another there may, therefore, be conflict between family responsibilities as they are defined in different cultures. Not all cultures define responsibility to others in the same way, and I will say more about this in Chapter 3. If a carer finds himself or herself caught between differing cultural expectations, then this is likely be a source of stress and dilemma.

From the point of view of providing help, this demands great sensitivity on the part of the helper and a willingness to look beyond your own cultural expectations. In fact, as a helper, you do not have to travel far outside your own cultural group to gain an understanding of these issues. Even within your own culture there will be a variety of sub-cultural beliefs and assumptions which reflect generational or class or gender or sexuality differences. Each sub-culture will have its own set of values and these too must be recognized and worked with. In general, if help is seen as an imposition of the values of one group or sub-group on another, then it simply cannot and will not be accepted and it is important for helpers to be aware of this.

Concluding Remarks

In summary, caring is a substantial task, both in terms of the numbers of carers within the population as a whole and in terms of the demands made on carers. Carers share many common experiences, such as the feeling that their distress is illegitimate and somehow less significant than that of the person cared for. This may lead to self-neglect and a variety of emotional reactions born of frustrated needs. Carers struggle to achieve a balance between responsibilities to others and to themselves. The extent to which they achieve this balance will influence how carers judge their success or failure in coping with their task.

Summary

❏ Carers constitute a significant proportion of any society.

❏ A list of typical characteristics of caring is described:
- the perceived illegitimacy by carers of their needs compared with the person cared for;
- the tendency towards self-denial and self-neglect;
- the fact that the caring role is often imposed rather than chosen;
- the disempowering effects of trying to relieve another's pain;
- the difficulties in adjusting to changes in pre-existing relationships with the person cared for;
- the uncertainty of the future.

❏ It is suggested that the above characteristics derive from social conventions and norms relating to the definition of good and poor care.

❏ A number of relationship models of care exist within any society. These include:
- a parental model;
- an offspring model;
- a partner model.

❏ The newly established *caring model* adopted by the carer will replace or supplement an existing relationship and this transition can be the cause of much distress.

❏ The carer model is some amalgam of the above relationship models and the carer's task is to adapt and adjust to the demands of the carer model.

❏ There can be a conflict of responsibilities and loyalties between the carer role and other roles in the carer's life and this will influence self-appraisal and, consequently, whether or not the carer copes.

❏ Race, ethnicity and culture are particularly potent sources of conventions and norms relating to caring and conflict may occur between the expectations of different generations who share the same ethnic roots but different cultural expectations.

❏ Helpers must be sensitive to differences between cultures and sub-cultures and avoid the imposition of one cultural definition of good care on another culture or sub-culture.

3

A Model of Coping

Chapter 2 was concerned with identifying the characteristics of caring. These were related to self-appraisal: the judgement carers make about how well or how badly they are coping with the task of caring in relation to the standards of care they hold. In this chapter I would like to take a look behind the scenes, so to speak, to examine what it is in the carer's experience that influences self-appraisal.

As we have already seen, when a person becomes a carer many changes take place in his or her life. The aim of the following will be to describe and illustrate some of the adjustments required. A framework from psychological theory will be provided within which to understand the nature of these adjustments. It is hoped that this will provide a context that will enable the helper to understand some of the reasons for, and circumstances underpinning, the difficulties experienced by carers.

A Framework for Understanding Difficulties in Coping

The framework adopted here is based on the social-cognitive approach described by numerous authors (Bandura, 1977; Abramson *et al.*, 1978; Lazarus *et al.*, 1980; Oatley and Bolton, 1985; Weiner, 1985 – see Brewin, 1988, for a comprehensive overview). For present purposes, this framework has at its centre three important concepts. The first is the *self*, with the associated notion of *self-esteem* or *self-worth*: the latter term will be used throughout. The second concept is *meaning*. The third is *access to resources*. This chapter looks in turn at the self and self-worth and the relational basis of human interaction; the concept of meaning as it is used in this text; and the assets which underlie and, therefore, define, successful or unsuccessful coping.

The Self

I have already alluded to self-appraisal in Chapter 2. I referred to the process of self-appraisal in which the carer asks himself or herself, 'How well am I doing my task of caring?' Coping is an evaluation of your actions in relation to a set of personal standards, such as the model or models of care adopted by the carer, which were described earlier. This is not an absolute judgement. What works for one person may not work for another. Equally, what works on one occasion may not work on another. Judgements of coping, therefore, are always relative to the individual and his or her circumstances at a particular time.

The notion of the self is central to understanding how a person copes. Guntrip (1971) writes widely about the nature of the self. In his view the self can be understood only in relation to other people. When we talk about the self, therefore, we are talking about 'whole selves in personal relationships, whose lives have meaning and value to them only in those terms' (p. 49). Some writers distinguish different aspects of the self, such as the private self, the public self and the collective self (Triandis, 1989). However, all aspects of the self are derived from relationships with other people. For Guntrip, there can be no self which exists in a vacuum, and this is the view that is followed in this book.

An important goal in human behaviour is to establish and maintain a positive view of your self and your actions. A characteristic of many people who have difficulty coping is that they have come to possess an impoverished sense of themselves: they feel impotent and unable to influence the world around them. As Beck (1976) has put it, they feel hopeless about themselves, the world and the future. It is essential, therefore, to establish and maintain self-worth. Self-worth, though, is not achieved in isolation from others. Much of our feeling about our own self-worth comes from the relationships we have. If someone values you, it enhances your self-worth. If someone dislikes you, then your self-worth may be threatened. If your self-worth is already low, then you will be relatively vulnerable to the negative reactions of others; if it is high, you will be more protected. Relationships, then, are the building blocks of self-worth. It will be apparent that if important relationships are lost or threatened through the illness or disability of a significant other, the integrity of self-worth may also be compromised.

The framework part I: conditions for maintaining self-worth

Following Brewin (1988), there are three important conditions for maintaining self-worth:

1. We should feel that our actual behaviour is consistent with the personal standards by which we define our ideal behaviour. If our behaviour fails to live up to those standards, then our self-worth will be diminished.
2. Our view of our own self should compare favourably with that of others we consider to be socially important to us.
3. When we consider our own behaviour, we should feel that it casts us in a favourable light.

I would also like to add a fourth, derived from Oatley and Bolton (1985):

4. In the face of loss, alternative and valued social roles contribute to the maintenance of self-worth. The absence of such alternatives compromises the ability to cope.

The above conditions provide a basis for understanding how problems may develop. They are likely to arise if any one of the above conditions are undermined. If the individual behaves in ways that are inconsistent with an ideal, or which do not conform to standards set by personally or socially relevant others, or if the explanation of behaviour is perceived as self-critical, or if a loss occurs which deprives a person of a valued role and no alternative role is available, then the person is likely to experience problems in coping.

Case example: a problem of self-worth

The example of Deirdre illustrates these points. For many years she had been a carer, but is now a widow following her partner's recent death. Even though her carer role has ceased, the example illustrates some of the demands she experienced when that role was still current, and how the process of adjustment continues even when the caring role no longer applies.

Deirdre, in her late sixties, had cared for her husband for ten years during his dementing illness. Although the task had been onerous, the necessity to get on with caring for her husband gave Deirdre a goal and a role that seemed to mitigate the difficulties she encountered. Despite the inevitable strains, Deirdre appeared to be coping. She never sought help and her general health remained good. The problems began when her husband died.

Following her husband's death a vacuum was created. Almost without realizing it, over the years the role of carer had become Deirdre's identity. With all its difficulties it was a role she valued and an extension of the role she had always occupied in the relationship before her husband's illness. The changes in the relationship following the illness had had the characteristics of a transition rather than an abrupt break. Now, however, the break occurred. Her husband's death, for all its predictability, was a shock. Furthermore, while the initial changes in her role at the beginning of her husband's illness had removed some options for her – for instance, she had to give up her work – others became available as a full-time carer. His death, though, left her with no further options. Life seemed pointless. To the surprise of many, the woman who had apparently coped so well with the stresses of looking after her husband, suddenly, on his death, became incapable of looking after herself. Deirdre was depressed and her doctor decided she needed help.

Deirdre's doctor was interested and had some training in helping skills. She recognized that the help needed by Deirdre required more than the usual brief appointment and so she arranged a series of special slots, on a weekly basis, to see Deirdre. She called these her 'counselling' slots. In these meetings they were able to discuss Deirdre's difficulties and identify the specific problems that existed. There seemed to be two major factors in Deirdre's depression. One was the natural reaction to the bereavement. The other, which compounded the first, was a hugely impaired sense of self-worth, manifest as self-blame for her husband's death. 'It was my fault,' she said. 'If only I had looked after him properly.' Not only was there self-blame for his death but also considerable self-criticism and despair: 'I was never any good. What's the point in going on?' The task of helping was to examine these depressive beliefs and gradually to disentangle them from the natural grief over her husband's death.

During the meetings it transpired that the relationship between Deirdre and her husband had always been characterized by Deirdre's need to care. She had married him, she said, because he needed someone to look after him. His illness had not brought about the dramatic change that it might have in other relationships. Rather it had merely accentuated a pattern that already existed.

In the meetings with her doctor, Deirdre was able to see that all her life she had never felt she could do enough: as a child, as a partner, as a carer. She had very high and quite unrealistic expectations of her behaviour towards others. She was able, for the first time, to acknowledge this characteristic. She made sense of it for herself in terms of the relationship she had had with her parents and her evolving self-belief that approval was never quite attainable and, therefore, she was never quite good enough. This striving for the unattainable became a personality characteristic and influenced her relationships with others, especially her husband. Yet the care she had provided had, in fact, been of a very high standard and with the help of the meetings with her doctor she was able to re-appraise her behaviour and her achievements. Eventually she began to accept that she had been more than just good enough and that her standards had been unrealistic. She had been her own strongest critic and she learnt that this was not now, and had never really been, necessary.

In terms of the criteria for the maintenance of self-worth identified above, it is apparent that:

- Deirdre failed to achieve consistency between actual and ideal behaviour, but this was because her ideals were unattainable.
- Her self did not compare favourably with socially important others. It never had, particularly with regard to her parents.
- Her explanations of her behaviour, in this case as a carer, did not, *in her mind*, cast a favourable light on her self-concept.
- On her husband's death she lost both her partner and the caring role she had occupied for a long time. Furthermore, no alternative role was available.

Deirdre's case is not untypical of other carers, whether or not they are still actively engaged in the task of caring. The point is that self-appraisal is a continual process for all of us, a normal process. As part of this normal process, the carer is constantly involved in tasks that may be judged satisfactory or unsatisfactory by his or her own standards. The outcome of these judgements affects the carer's sense of self and this directly influences coping. If the judgement is consistently negative, the carer will feel he or she is failing and vice versa. Coping, then, depends upon a positive outcome of self-appraisal and the correspondingly positive self-worth that ensues from that appraisal.

The Meaning of Behaviour

Self-worth is a product of the relationship between an individual and his or her world. It is derived from judgements made by an individual about his or her behaviour in relation to people and circumstances. The process of making such judgements is one aspect of a wider enterprise concerned with attributing *meaning* to events and behaviour. The basic assumption here is that people attempt to make sense of their worlds. When an event occurs, the individual will endeavour to work out why the event took place: what was the cause and what are the consequences? He or she may also wish to know how long it is likely to last, who was responsible and how wide will be its impact. The answers found to these questions will determine how the person responds to the event and this too will influence how he or she copes. The meaning of the event is, therefore, another factor which is critical in defining self-worth.

These are not just theoretical concerns. They are accompanied by emotions: fear, anxiety, anger, despair, helplessness, hopelessness, rage, guilt, shame. The meaning of the event to the carer – its causes and consequences – underpins these emotions. For instance, carers often admit feelings of guilt about their relative's illness: 'If only I had looked after him better,' or 'I was never there, always busy, always finding some reason not to be at home with her.' Such statements reveal potential guilt and a belief that they, the carers, might have contributed, however indirectly, to the other's illness or deterioration. This, in turn, is bound to affect the relationship between the carer and person cared for.

The question is: how do such thoughts and feelings affect the carer's capacity to cope with caring? At best they are a natural part of the process of adjustment by the carer to the changes wrought by illness or injury in the person cared for. At worst, however, if they persist and become an established belief, they can certainly handicap both the carer and the person cared for. This brings us to the second part of the framework within which we shall aim to understand the problems of caring.

The framework part II: a model of the meaning of events

The model is derived from Weiner's (1985) theory of motivation and emotion. The theory aims to explain how and why people

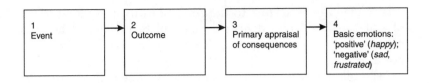

Figure 1 The first four stages in the model of a carer's search for the meaning of the events that have led to the caring role.

experience specific emotions following a particular event. The model is presented in stages. As a comparison, the stages might be likened to a film that has been frozen, frame by frame. Played at full speed, the different stages merge into a seamless and continuous whole. For the purposes of illustration, however, they are presented here as separate stages.

Imagine the following scenario. Your partner, or parent, or child has an illness which leads to an incapacity and a need for long-term care. You are shocked by the unexpected occurrence of this event and its implications and you try to work out why and how it occurred. You seek a causal explanation and the reasons you identify – the sense you make of it all – will influence how you cope subsequently. The first four of the eight stages in the model are illustrated in Figure 1.

(1) An *event* takes place, for instance an accident or an illness in a partner or parent or child.

(2) This has an *outcome*, which is perceived, or suspected, or feared, such as disability and/or pain in a partner, parent or child, although the outcome may not be apparent immediately. In the initial stages the outcome may be what is suspected, or feared to be the case, rather than what will, ultimately, turn out to be the case.

(3) There is a *primary appraisal* of the *consequences* of the event: an initial reaction. A common consequence for new carers relates to *change and potential loss of role*. This may become manifested as a sense of abandonment, or desertion, or powerlessness. However it manifests, there is a basic recognition that a gap has occurred in the previous relationship the person had with the person concerned. Something that once was there is no longer. For carers, the primary appraisal would be one of change: their role is and will be different. The implications of

this change can be related to the conditions for the preservation of self-worth already identified and will be further elaborated below when the *meaning of the consequences* is considered (see point 5).

(4) Following the primary appraisal, *basic emotions* are triggered in the carer. Once again, these are an initial reaction, a kind of first impression. The emotions are perceived by the carer to be either *positive* or *negative* in terms of their assumed adaptive consequences and occur automatically, without conscious reflection. The basic emotions have been described by Weiner as broadly *happy* on the adaptively positive side and *sad* and *frustrated* on the adaptively negative side. This gives the primary emotional colour to the event, which will influence the form of the more complex emotions that follow.

However, the subsequent complex emotions are not always consonant with this primary response. For instance, if you hear you are to be offered promotion at work, the primary emotional response may be broadly *happy*. However, as the implications become clearer the emotions may change. If, say, promotion means re-location, a new house with more financial commitment, new schools for the children, losing friends, taking on onerous responsibility at work and so forth, you might become apprehensive and feel more negative about the prospect. This is an example of the way in which apparently positive events such as promotion can be just as stressful as more obviously negative events. In the same way, an apparently negative event might, on reflection, have many positive aspects. For instance, apparently negative frustration may be the basis for highly motivated, and therefore positive, problem-solving behaviour. Similarly, apparently negative sadness may act as a means of rehearsal for the profound feelings associated with a loss that has occurred and, therefore, be adaptively positive in the long run.

(5) As the fact of the event registers, the *meaning of the consequences* begins to be considered by the carer (Figure 2), leading to questions such as: 'Why me?', 'Why now?', 'How did it happen?', 'How will my life be affected?', 'How long will it last?' For example, if the carer is the spouse of the person cared for, he or she may have had a sense of *self as partner* before the event, a relationship that incorporated roles such as *lover* and *confidant*, with *shared interests*. The carer also had roles outside the relationship and operated in a *social environment*. After the event all these roles are affected; the balance is changed. A

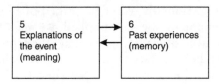

Figure 2 The fifth and sixth stages in the model of a carer's search for the meaning of the events that have led to the caring role.

similar change occurs in relationships where the person cared for is a child. The balance of the relationship between the parents is also disturbed and not all marriages survive the new stresses of caring. In particular, as some new roles evolve, others will be lost. The implications of loss of role are fundamental to the ways in which the carer will cope and the new role of carer may not always be a valued alternative to the lost role as partner or parent, with all the associated benefits and satisfactions. Thus the conditions for the preservation of self-worth described earlier may become undermined at this stage.

One important part of this process of searching for meaning is the attribution of cause. If the event was an illness in one's partner, parent or child, what caused the illness? Was it something *external* – an accident, fate, chance? Or was it something *internal* – my neglect in the relationship, my wrong decision, my wrong choice? Was I responsible? This is termed the *locus* of the event. In addition, other causal attributions include *stability* – how long will it last? – and *controllability* – do I have any control over events?

The answers the carer finds to all these questions can have a profound impact on subsequent coping or not coping. For example, if the carer blames himself or herself, then the consequent guilt will shape the course of the relationship between carer and the person cared for. We cannot easily predict how that relationship will develop. It may, for instance, lead to an over-solicitous, over-protective relationship as the carer attempts to make up for perceived past misdemeanours. On the other hand, it could equally cause distance between the carer and person cared for, as the former is unable to face up to the consequences of his or her perceived culpability. As helpers, in order to achieve any understanding of this process, we need to discover the questions the carer has asked of himself or herself, and the answers he or she has supplied: we need to ascertain the carer's attribution of cause. This may then provide a key to understanding how a particular pattern of behaviour has developed between the carer and the person cared for.

(6) The basic answers the carer finds for his or her questions are informed by *memory* of similar events. Has such an event happened before? If so, why did it happen then? What does that *past experience* tell me about this present event? If there is no direct personal experience, is there any indirect experience based on my knowledge of others in such circumstances?

(7) *Complex emotions* are then generated, which reflect the nature of the explanation that has been worked out by the individual carer (Figure 3). These are a development of the basic emotions described earlier and, as mentioned before, the complex emotions are not necessarily consonant with the earlier, basic emotions. An example of a complex emotion would be *anger* or *rage*, which may stem from the belief that someone or something was responsible for negatively perceived consequences. The anger may be *self-directed* and associated with personal *guilt* and *shame*, or *other-directed* and associated with another's culpability. In turn, that other may be the partner, child or parent, or may be someone else with whom the person

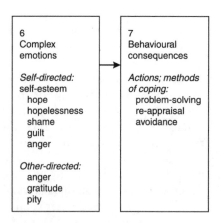

Figure 3 The seventh and eighth stages in the model of a carer's search for the meaning of the events that have led to the caring role.

cared for has had dealings: a supervisor at work who neglected safety regulations, or a doctor responsible for medical care that was perceived as neglectful, and so forth. It will be apparent that the attributions made by the carer will have a direct effect on self-concept and are more or less likely to threaten self-worth according to the nature of the explanation and the complex emotions that follow.

One of the most common problems for carers arises from the difficulty that can be experienced in expressing the complex emotions directly. For example, a carer may be angry with health-care staff because he or she believes, rightly or wrongly, that their actions have in some way contributed to, or exacerbated, or been insufficient to deal with, the problem. However, the carer and the person cared for may remain heavily reliant on the same health-care staff for future treatment, so that the direct expression of anger is impossible without, they believe, compromising future care. Similar constraints may inhibit the true expression of emotions between carer and the person cared for. The reliance of one on the other can be perceived as an obstacle which necessitates inhibiting real feelings. When feelings are inhibited in this way they can simmer and fester inside the individual and assume a scale that is entirely out of proportion to the original event. In addition, they cause a great deal of psychological distress and dysfunction to the individual so afflicted. Examples of the effects on a person of the inhibition of emotions will be provided later.

(8) Finally, the emotional response underlies *actions* made in response to the event. These actions are the basis for *coping* or *not coping*. The combination of explanations and emotions constitute the *meaning* of the total experience which underpins self-appraisal and governs the coping actions undertaken by the carer. Coping, in turn, provides feedback about personal efficacy and further influences the sense of self-worth that develops in relation to the task in hand.

Coping in the Longer Term – Access to Resources

Coping has so far been defined as a certain kind of psychological response to events in which self-worth is not undermined or threatened by the trauma and disruption that has occurred in the process of becoming a carer. For all of the transient self-doubts, uncertainties and profound emotions of loss, if the conditions for the maintenance of self-worth are preserved, ultimately the carer will be likely to cope. However, I have already likened the task of caring to what Frankl (1959) termed *a provisional existence*: a task of uncertain duration and unpredictable demands. Self-worth, then, can continue to be threatened and compromised by future adversity. The carer in his or her new role will encounter many difficulties in adapting to these new circumstances and the evolving relationship with the person cared for is not fixed but will change with time. It is very important, if the carer is to maintain a sense of coping, that he or she has access to a variety of necessary resources.

The framework part III: coping in the longer term – access to resources

According to Knussen and Cunningham (1988, p. 338) the ability to cope involves having available:

1. physical assets, such as health, energy and stamina;
2. social assets, such as social networks and support systems;
3. psychological assets, such as beliefs and values, problem-solving skills, self-worth and morale;
4. material assets, such as money, equipment and tools.

I will provide a detailed account in the next chapter of the sorts of needs carers report in relation to these resources. For the present, it is sufficient to note that the lack of the above assets can compromise carers' ability to cope.

Coping, then, depends on the carer's personal psychological response to the event that has led to the carer role and the success or difficulty experienced in maintaining self-worth. But it would be a mistake to give the impression that successful coping depends only on the personal psychological response of the carer. Even the most psychologically robust individual can flounder if the basic assets are not available. Caring is a fluid task which evolves and develops and the carer must also have access to resources in order to maintain his or her coping.

For the *helper*, the task is to understand as far as possible the personal reaction to the event and how this may have influenced coping and, in addition, to be aware of the importance of appropriate resources. Helping carers to cope, therefore, entails the helper, in collaboration with carers, first identifying and then addressing any deficits in the psychological and material coping resources and devising strategies which will potentially restore the balance. This task will be examined in detail in the following chapters.

Concluding Remarks

I have attempted, in this chapter, to provide quite a complex model of the process of coping. Coping is defined as the case where the sense of self-worth is maintained or enhanced and there is access to appropriate resources. Difficulty in coping occurs when the sense of self-worth is threatened and diminished and there are resource deficits. The meaning of the task of caring, on the one hand, and the strategies adopted in the task of caring, on the other, will influence the success or otherwise of the enterprise.

As I said earlier, each component or stage in the model is like an individual frozen frame in a film. In reality, the stages merge into each other in a continuous process, many parts of which take place unconsciously. What we, as helpers, will see when we are faced with a carer experiencing problems is the *product* of this seamless process. From the product we can begin to infer the underlying components of the process and in so doing begin to help the carer move from a position of not coping to one of coping. The means by which we can enable this change will be the subject of the following chapters. I hope that the present chapter will have provided some additional context to understand the nature of the problems that carers face and that we, as helpers, will be addressing in our helping role.

Summary

❑ Coping derives from *self-appraisal* and depends on the maintenance of *self-worth*.

❑ Self-worth is a product of the relationship between an individual and his or her world.

❑ Carers experience a number of emotions in response to the task of caring. The theory is described of the route from the initial event which leads to the carer role to the complex emotions that are experienced as a result.

❑ Carers search for the *meaning* and *implications* of what has happened to them and the person cared for. The answers they find will determine how they cope.

❑ It is suggested that the *helper* needs to identify the meaning of the event to the carer in order to understand the carer's attribution of cause. This then provides an insight into the carer's self-appraisal and any subsequent difficulties in coping.

❑ The relationship between carer and the person cared for is not fixed and as it evolves the carer will need access to a variety of resources.

❑ Coping is defined as a combination of the carer's personal psychological response to the event and the availability of resources required to maintain coping.

❑ Helping carers to cope is a collaborative enterprise between helper and carer. The aim is first to identify and then to address any deficits in the psychological and material coping resources of the carer and devise strategies for rectifying these.

4

What Needs Do Carers Have?

Bearing in mind the characteristics of caring described in Chapter 2 and the process of coping or not coping described in Chapter 3, I would now like to examine in more detail the subject of carers' needs. The range of needs is extensive and includes the practical, emotional, treatment, social, spiritual and intellectual aspects of the carer's life. In order to appreciate the nature of these needs fully it is helpful to elucidate further those features that distinguish carers as a population from others who may seek help but are not engaged in the task of caring.

The first point to make is that there is what I will term a *standard view* of helping and help-seeking and that carers do not always subscribe to this. Because the standard view is widely held among certain of the established helping professions, such as counsellors, psychiatrists, psychotherapists and clinical psychologists, it may already influence the helper's assumptions about what is required to help carers.

A central feature of the standard view of helping, as described in the counselling and psychological therapy literature, is the precondition that there should be a recognition by the client of the need for help and a consequent motivation to change. According to this view, clients seek help because they face problems that are overwhelming or difficult to cope with alone. However, it is not enough just to want help. The help-seeker must also want to change his or her behaviour in relation to the problems encountered. It is suggested that without the basic ingredients of recognizing the need for help and wanting to change, helping cannot proceed. Skills cannot be imposed on reluctant or passive clients and, even if they could, they would be unlikely to bring about valued changes.

The evidence in relation to carers, though, is that this standard view is not always appropriate. Several attempts have been made to provide formal counselling for carers along the lines defined by the standard view. For instance, in the UK, in response to the government's 'Care in the Community' proposals, one nationally established counselling service offered to incorporate a carer counselling project within its existing organization. Unfortunately, the experiment was not a success. Quite understandably in the circumstances, the organizers offered the standard arrangement whereby sessions were offered to carers in the organization's offices, away from the carers' homes, with all the problems of travel and time away from caring this involved. These arrangements reflect the standard assumption that if people are truly motivated to change then they will find a way to overcome the practical difficulties in attending sessions. However, the overwhelming response from carers was that this was unworkable. Attending counselling sessions was perceived by carers to conflict with their prime responsibility to care. Eventually, the scheme folded (Twigg, 1992).

This raises an important issue for the helper. Helping professionals are used to organizing the delivery of help in a way that reflects the priorities of the organizations in which they work and is consistent with the standard view described above. Thus help, in general, is often presented as something out of the ordinary, for which carers are expected to make special arrangements, reflecting the priorities they give to the help sought. Carers, on the other hand, often describe their priorities not in terms of a personal need for counselling or therapy, but in terms of practical needs, primarily for the person cared for, but sometimes also for themselves. It will be apparent that if the helper's assumptions are incompatible with the carer's needs, then problems are likely to arise. Thus the first two distinguishing characteristics of carers are:

1. Carers may not always subscribe to traditional assumptions about the conditions for seeking help.
2. The difficulties for which carers seek help may not directly be the carer's; often the difficulties are perceived primarily to be those of the person cared for.

It follows from this that there are two kinds of help that can apply to carers:

1. Direct help for the carer, for his or her own needs.

2. Indirect help, via the carer, for the needs of the person cared for.

In addition, there are three overlapping forms of help that may be offered to carers. These are:

1. information and advice on practical matters such as financial support, mobility aids and voluntary or statutory organizations which may be able to provide further help;
2. material and emotional support, which may take the form of increased contact with others in order to decrease social isolation – for instance, membership of carers' organizations and support groups – or it may involve respite, for both the carer and the person cared for;
3. problem-solving, which refers to the development of skills which will enable the carer, or, in some cases, the person cared for, to identify and then deal more effectively with a specific problem or range of problems.

Although these types of help overlap, it is important for the helper to be clear about what kind of help is primarily being requested. The options are represented in Table 1.

Table 1 What is the principal focus of help?

	Information and advice	Support (e.g. respite care)	Problem-solving
Person cared for			
Carer			

The initial focus may be on one aspect of help, but later in the helping process other needs may become apparent. Alternatively, a variety of needs may be apparent from the start.

A related issue that distinguishes carers from other populations seeking help is the question of *outcome*, or the goals of helping. Professional helping is effective only insofar as it leads to *valued outcomes* for the person being helped (Egan, 1990). One potential complication in helping carers is that there may be a discrepancy or even a conflict between outcomes for the carer and the person cared for. A valued outcome for the carer may, for instance, be less time with the person cared for. In contrast, a valued outcome for the person cared for might be more time. This raises the question of whose interest the helper is serving. The helper may enable the carer to reduce stress by spending less time with the person cared for, and then the latter becomes more distressed. The same issue arises if help is primarily directed to the person cared for but leaves the carer with increased demands and responsibilities. Thus a further distinguishing characteristic of carers is:

- the definition of a valued outcome of helping may be unclear or ambiguous.

It should be noted that such dilemmas are not necessarily founded upon a direct conflict of self-interest between carer and person cared for. For example, the carer may want to spend the maximum time possible with the person cared for, but the price may be intolerable stress, leading to ill health in the carer and difficulties in coping. In this case, the carer may require help in acknowledging that it is in the longer-term interest of all concerned that he or she has some respite from the task of caring.

In summary, any one individual may have multiple needs and potentially benefit from more than one type of help. Set up in the correct way, a carer may begin by acknowledging the need for, and receiving, one form of help, such as practical advice and information, or respite care. Having benefited from this, he or she may then become aware of the other types of available help and decide to explore these. Clearly, such an informed choice, initiated by the carer, is more likely to succeed than approaches which are based on assumptions about carers' needs, derived from a standard view of helping.

Carers' Needs

Bearing in mind the above points, let us now consider the nature of carers' needs more specifically. The carer's task has a number of aspects. Grad and Sainsbury (1965) have distinguished between the carer's *objective burden* and the *subjective burden*. While maintaining this distinction, I believe the terms *material burden* and *emotional burden* respectively are more descriptive. In addition, I think it is possible to discern a further aspect of the carer's task to do with the *personal relationship* between carer and person cared for. These aspects of the carer's task are common across cultures. However, there are cultural differences in the communication of distress, attitudes to help-seeking, and the provision of help, and I will also address these issues in this chapter.

Although I will discuss all these aspects separately, it must be remembered that they are all parts of the same entity: namely the task of providing care for another. Clearly, each is linked. The material burden is likely to have emotional consequences. Similarly, an emotional burden can undermine the carer's capacity to cope and this can have detrimental material consequences. Both are influenced by the relationship between carer and person cared for. The point is that carers have a variety of needs specific to the task of caring and the deficits which they represent are a cause of substantial distress. Helpers are often faced with the manifest distress and must recognize the carer's needs that underpin it.

Factors that affect levels of distress in carers are described by a number of authors (Compton *et al.*, 1997; Matson, 1994; Twigg and Atkin, 1994; Morris *et al.*, 1991; Brodarty and Hadzi-Pavlovic, 1990; Gilleard *et al.*, 1984a,b; Gilhooly, 1984) and can be divided into the three broad perspectives just described. I will deal with each aspect of carers' needs in turn.

Characteristics of the Relationship Between Carer and Person Cared For

Gender of the carer and person cared for

Morris *et al.* (1991) report the common finding that female carers suffer a greater burden than male carers. It has been argued that women are more likely to be socialized into the role of carer and, in a family setting where there are a number of offspring of a relative requiring care, it is likely to be the female who ends up as the carer.

It is also reported that the stress of caring is increased where the carer lives with the person cared for and although this would apply both to men and women, there appear to be more cases of daughters living with and caring for a frail elderly parent than sons. If the task involves a parent caring for a son or daughter, then in many societies it is more often the mother who acts as the primary carer and the father who maintains a link with the outside world through work. The woman, therefore, may have less relief from caring, less variety and less contact with the outside world, and this adds to her burden.

There is also some evidence of gender differences in coping styles. While men and women as individuals may have a variety of coping styles, it is reported that women in general report they feel less in control of the task of caring than men (Barusch and Spaid, 1989). These authors also reported that male carers felt more in control of the material problems of caring, while females felt more successful at coping with the emotional aspects of caring.

Having said all of this, it is important to emphasize that each carer should be treated as an individual. Helpers must avoid being influenced by stereotypical assumptions about what it must be like to be a carer; they must listen to each carer on an individual basis. The above generalizations may be useful as a starting point, but can never tell the whole story.

The quality of the previous relationship between carer and the person cared for

If the relationship between the carer and person cared for was poor before their new roles began, then the task of caring is likely to be complicated by unresolved differences and conflicts. The carer may harbour feelings of anger, guilt or resentment towards the person cared for, and this will become manifest in the new, dependent, relationship.

Mrs B, who suffered dementia, lived with her son and daughter-in-law. The relationship between Mrs B and her son had always been strained. She had always been a figure of authority to her son and he had been frightened of her as a child. Now, as she grew older, the balance of power in the relationship changed. Mrs B had become very forgetful and easily confused. One day she attempted to put the electric kettle on the gas cooker and had to be restrained from doing so by her son: the more he tried to stop her, the more she was determined to do it. After a short while, she became enraged and abusive and attacked him. He, in turn, became enraged himself and hit her.

It is thought that many cases of so-called 'elder abuse' derive from such circumstances. For instance, Compton *et al.* (1997)

found that in cases of abuse of elderly people with dementia, there had previously been a higher incidence of verbal or physical abuse or other problem behaviours by the person cared for towards the carer.

Nature and severity of the disturbance in the person cared for

One of the main influences on carer stress is reported to be the extent of disruptive behaviour in the person cared for (Coen *et al.*, 1997). This is a greater cause of stress for carers than physical disability or intellectual impairment in the person cared for. For example, carers report greater distress themselves if the person they care for is prone to wander away from a safe environment, and endanger himself or herself and others, or engage in behaviour that causes social embarrassment and/or danger to the person cared for, such as sexualized behaviour or aggression.

Mrs C's husband had suddenly become sexually disinhibited, following a head injury. He would go up to a complete stranger in the street or a shop and make overt sexual advances, touching and fondling. On one occasion he was arrested and it was only after extreme pleading by his wife that he was released without charge. Her distress, embarrassment and humiliation were, of course, considerable, and she sought professional help, through her physician, to try to gain some control over this deteriorating situation.

In such cases both the carer and the person cared for need specialist professional advice from a clinical psychologist or a behaviourally orientated health professional.

The Material Burden of Caring

Material difficulties such as financial hardship and poor housing

The material burden refers to the material costs of caring, its effects on the carer's employment, financial status, housing and other material resources. For example, if the carer has to give up work in order to provide care, then there will be consequences for his or her finances. In some cases there may be financial support, such as grants for equipment and adaptations to the home. These may be from government bodies or charitable foundations. In some countries there are specific carer benefits, such as an attendance allowance, and the person cared for may also be eligible for some form of disability allowance or other financial support. It is important that helpers should become familiar with their local system, the sources of information and advice, the statutory and non-statutory organizations. It is helpful to know where to find relevant information and advice on this. Many of the carers' organizations that have been formed to support those caring for people with specific conditions can also give advice in relation to common problems found among the relevant population. Thus much of the material burden can be addressed with appropriate information and advice, although many carers find that there are continuing material hardships despite receiving all available help, advice and benefits.

Practical help with aids around the home and other resources

If the person cared for has physical disabilities, then a variety of physical aids may be available (a stair-lift, changes to the bathroom or kitchen, re-housing). Usually the local social services are the first point of contact for information about these. Local health services (a physician, occupational therapist, physiotherapist, or other health professional) may also be able to provide information and guidance. Alternatively some countries have advice bureaux and voluntary organizations, or there may be information in libraries about relevant resources.

Information and advice on practical problems, such as incontinence, behavioural difficulties and general physical care

It is said that knowledge is power. The antithesis of this is that ignorance creates impotence. If a carer feels powerless to perform his or her task of caring, then we have a basis for difficulties in coping. Information by itself is not sufficient to guarantee coping altogether, but it is one of the main necessary ingredients for alleviating some of the material burden of caring. Information and advice will equip the carer to cope more effectively and to know where to go for further help. He or she may, in addition, need other forms of support as well, but without basic information it is difficult even to begin to cope.

The task for the helper, then, is to facilitate coping by providing information and advice where necessary. The provision of knowledge is a form of empowerment which enables the carer to make decisions and choices and, in general terms, reduces the stress associated with uncertainty. It is important, therefore, for you as a helper to know where certain kinds of information are available and to be able either to provide it yourself, or to direct the carer to the source of relevant information. Once again, carers' organizations, where they exist, are particularly useful. Most libraries or advice centres will have a list of relevant national and local carers' organizations. Advice on practical problems such as incontinence, behavioural difficulties and general physical care is usually within the province of health and social care professionals, such as specialist nurses, doctors and clinical psychologists.

The Emotional Burden

There is substantial evidence of emotional distress among carers. Studies of carers whose dependants are attending statutory services such as psychiatric outpatient clinics, day hospitals for the elderly and general hospital services reveal much emotional distress, although the numbers of carers affected vary. Prevalence rates range from about a third (e.g. Oldridge and Hughes, 1992) through about 50% (e.g. Gilleard *et al.*, 1984b) to about 75% (Scottish Schizophrenia Research Group, 1985; Gibbons *et al.*, 1984). Even at the lower estimates, the rates are twice those to be expected within the general population (Wing, 1981, cited in Oldridge and Hughes, 1992). We must assume that the variability in the reported rates of emotional distress is due to differences in the magnitude of the carer's task, the amount of time he or she has been responsible for the task of caring and the personal resources of the carer. In addition, the amount and type of support available to the carer confers protection from the stresses of caring. Oldridge and Hughes (1992) suggest that studies reporting lower rates of distress may involve carers who receive relatively better support than those reporting higher rates.

Caring for the dependent other at home

Most of us move in and out of different environments from time to time: home, work, social life, extended family. The variety of different environments can be stimulating, interesting and rewarding. If some environments are stressful, such as the work environment, then we need a balance to compensate for this and provide an antidote to stress. In particular, for many people, home provides a sanctuary from the stresses of everyday existence. It will be apparent, then, that if home is where the task of caring takes place, the balance is changed. Home no longer represents a haven, but is the location associated with the greatest stresses. Furthermore, the task of caring may preclude the opportunity to find variety and stimulation in environments outside the home. In these circumstances it is not surprising if the carer becomes isolated and demoralized, with all the concomitant emotions of irritation and anger or hopelessness and depression.

Lack of support for the carer

Caring for another restricts the carer's social and work options. The result can be increased isolation from friends, family and the world at large. Isolation ultimately may lead to a loss of confidence and an increased likelihood of social withdrawal by the carer in the longer term. Helpers may be one of the few sources of contact *for the carer* with the world outside caring. Carers' organizations also fulfil an important role in this respect by providing national or local networks for carers. As well as all the practical help afforded by such organizations, their social role should not be underestimated. Carers often experience great relief when they come into contact with a carers' organization and discover that there are other people who experience similar demands and difficulties. Feeling that one is alone in dealing with a difficult task can be very demoralizing and helpers, whether professionals within the health and social services, or volunteers from carers' organizations, can contribute to dispelling this illusion.

The carer's poor health

In an important study of the effects of stress on the immune system, Kiercolt-Glaser *et al.* (1991) examined the health and illness of carers of a person with Alzheimer's disease. They found that, in general, the husbands or wives of someone with Alzheimer's disease more often suffered infectious illness than is found in a population of men and women of the same age and from the same social circumstances. Furthermore, the less social support the carers reported, the more physically ill and emotionally depressed they were. In general, carers as a whole were more socially isolated than non-carers and felt more helpless and distressed than non-carers. Other researchers have confirmed these findings (McCann, 1991; Irwin *et al.*, 1991; Pomara *et al.*, 1989) and it seems reasonable to conclude that what is true for carers of people with Alzheimer's disease is also true for carers of people with any kind of illness or disability, inasmuch that the carers are exposed to comparable kinds of stress.

Thus any individual carer who is isolated or who suffers material deprivation is more vulnerable than average to illness and emotional distress. The task of struggling unabatedly with extreme practical and emotional demands will tax the resources of the strongest individual. The consequences of such difficulties depend on their magnitude, chronicity and the personal resources of the carer. A carer who is under stress and whose health is impaired is under an increased emotional burden and will, therefore, be less able to deal effectively with the task of caring.

Individual coping styles adopted by carers

It is clear from the evidence described so far that the task of caring is onerous and that it can create material and emotional difficulties for carers. However, it is also clear that the impact of these difficulties is moderated by such characteristics as the nature and magnitude of the caring task, the relationship between the carer and person cared for, the support available to the carer and the past coping experience of the carer.

The past coping experience of the carer, or *coping style*, is an important influence on how effectively she or he copes. Coping styles range from passive avoidance, at one end of the continuum, to active problem-solving at the other. Most use strategies that fall somewhere between the extremes and vary from problem-solving in some circumstances to avoidance in others.

In general, the tendency towards avoidance *as a long-term strategy* is a sign of failing to cope. We all have bad days and may avoid things when these occur. However, if avoidance becomes habitual, then problems begin to pile up. The balance, in the long term, must be towards the active, problem-solving end of the spectrum if the carer is to cope effectively. I will be saying more about this later in the book. For the present it is worth noting that there is evidence that the experience of coping in the past will influence how effectively the carer copes with his or her current task of caring. If there has been a history of difficulties in coping in a range of circumstances before becoming a carer, then this is likely to generalize to the task of caring. The helper, therefore, would do well to ask the carer about this and gain an impression of what coping skills the carer may already have, or may lack.

Coping skills can sometimes be present in the carer but be obscured by a temporary difficulty. In this case, the carer may be helped to rediscover his or her temporarily misplaced skills. The carer may be likened to someone in a foreign land without a map. The helper's task is to provide direction so that the carer is enabled to take control and plan his or her route autonomously. If those skills are poorly developed, however, and the carer has always experienced some difficulty in coping, then the helper's task is different and may involve enabling the carer to learn and establish those skills necessary for more effective coping in the longer term.

Culture, Ethnicity and Carers' Needs

I have already referred in Chapter 2 to cultural and ethnic differences in the definition of appropriate relationships between carers and those cared for. I have also referred to differences between carers as a population compared with others seeking help and described problems with what I termed the standard view of helping as presented in the counselling and psychological therapy literature. Similar issues arise with respect to differences among carers from different cultures or ethnic groups. The basic question is what similarities or differences, if any, are there between carers from different cultural or ethnic backgrounds, and what implications, if any, might these have for the task of helping carers?

There are four broad issues relating to culture and ethnicity:

1. similarities and differences in the needs of carers from different cultural and ethnic groups;
2. similarities and differences in attitudes to seeking and receiving help;
3. similarities and differences in the communication of distress;
4. cultural variation in the means by which help may be provided.

Looking at the first of these, there is evidence that needs are very similar across groups. McCalman (1990) has provided a helpful overview of the needs of three groups resident in the UK which will also be relevant to other minority groups within other societies. The groups are African-Caribbean, Asian and Vietnamese/Chinese carers. McCalman describes carers in these ethnic groups as 'the forgotten people', reflecting how little is known about the needs of these groups within the wider UK society. Perhaps the most important conclusion from her research is that carers from minority ethnic groups in the UK have comparable experiences to carers from the majority ethnic groups. They also, therefore, have comparable needs.

Often there are material differences in terms of poverty, housing and racism, but these factors seem less influential than a basic lack of awareness, both among carers about what services may be available to them, and also among providers of services who may be unaware of the general needs of minority groups. In addition, there may be a problem of language: clearly, a shared language is fundamental to seeking and providing help and this is often not available.

Nevertheless, the evidence suggests that carers from a variety of ethnic and cultural groups have essentially the same needs as carers in the rest of society. The full range of advice and information is required on respite care, benefits, day centres and the variety of helps and aids available to those in need. Lack of a shared language and shared idioms may be a substantial barrier to seeking and receiving help, but this can be overcome with culturally sensitive information and help. A number of carers' organizations now provide information in a range of languages. In addition, some organizations have multi-lingual helpers.

With respect to the question of ethnic and cultural differences in attitudes to seeking and receiving help, it is apparent that differences do exist and these have important implications for helpers involved in providing help to carers. McCalman (1990) writes: 'The Asian community expected elderly relatives to be cared for by their families and any intervention from outsiders was seen as a social disgrace.' The same attitudes were not prominent in the other groups studied. These differences reflect a broad issue of cultural convention.

As I have already mentioned in Chapter 2, in any community there are norms which determine what is perceived as 'good' care. Different communities may vary in their definitions of these norms. Thus, in one community outside help may have connotations of failure, whereas in another outside help may be seen as a right. Such culturally determined attitudes towards the meaning of outside help will also determine whether help is or is not sought in the first place. This, of course, presents a challenge to helpers who do not wish to demean those who need help. The helper needs to be sensitive to these potential differences and wherever necessary seek advice from someone or some organization familiar with the conventions and beliefs of the culture in question.

Looking now at the communication of distress, here too differences can be found among cultures. A major issue that will affect the task of helping is the question of the language or idiom with which emotional distress is communicated. Cultures often differ in the language used to express distress and there is a tendency in western societies to use psychological language, which is not always found among non-western societies. For instance, Chinese medicine, while recognizing emotional disturbance, describes it in physical terms (e.g. Wu, 1982). Similarly, in Iranian society (Good and Good, 1982) and Punjabi society (Krause, 1989) distress may be expressed in physical rather than psychological terms.

The latter two cases provide a good example of a point that applies more generally to a range of cultures. In both Iranian and Punjabi societies emotional difficulties are expressed by reference to disturbances of the heart. Good and Good refer to 'heart distress' among indigenous Iranians. Krause describes the idiom of the 'sinking heart', which is used to convey distress among Punjabi immigrants to the UK. In both cases, the person complains of physical pain or discomfort in the heart (pounding, squeezing, quivering), in the absence of any actual physical disorder. In effect, when a Punjabi man or woman complains of physical debility in terms of a sinking heart, he or she is using a physical expression as an idiom for emotional distress. Similarly, the Iranian expression of heart distress is an idiom for emotional disturbance. The response from a helper must, therefore, take account of the idiomatic use of language and the underlying message being conveyed.

Clearly, not all helpers will have the knowledge and experience to recognize such idioms, and if your work brings you into contact with a variety of ethnic and cultural groups, it is essential to seek advice and information from someone familiar with the community in question. I must stress, though, that it is one thing to recognize cultural idioms for the expression of emotion, but it does not follow that it is always appropriate to challenge them. There is a place for challenging another's preconceptions and I will say more about this later in the book. But in relation to other ethnic communities, we must avoid any kind of cultural imperialism that implies that one cultural perspective is somehow better or more appropriate than another. At the risk of parody, it would be disastrous to respond to someone from another ethnic community by saying: 'No, no, it is not your heart, it is your emotions that are the problem.' A helper may view the problem in precisely these terms, but the issue is not 'Whose idiom is right?', but 'How can I help?' The term *alienation* seems to suggest itself here. If we treat someone from another ethnic community as an alien, then he or she will become alienated, and that will preclude our best attempts to help.

Finally, with respect to the provision of help, it is important to acknowledge that different cultures value different aspects of human behaviour and this has implications for the task of helping. In order to understand this it is necessary to refer again to the *self-concept*. I have referred in Chapters 1 and 2 to the importance of self-appraisal in determining whether a carer judges himself or herself to be coping with the task of caring. As I have already suggested, this self-appraisal is based on an internal model of how the individual feels he or she *ought to behave* in relation to others; and these models are derived from conventions and norms within the particular society in question. The fact is, though, that there are differences between cultures in which particular aspect of the self is deemed to be of primary importance. Thus self-appraisal must be understood in relation to which aspect of the self is being appraised.

This point is illustrated by Triandis (1989), who distinguishes three aspects of self-concept. These are:

1. *the private self*, or assessment of yourself *by* yourself: ' I am ... honest, introverted, brave, ... etc.'
2. *the public self*, or assessment of yourself in relation to a generalized other: 'People think I am ... honest ... etc.'
3. *the collective self*, or assessment of yourself in relation to a specific reference group: 'My family/colleagues/friends etc. think I am ... honest ... etc.'

Different cultures emphasize different aspects of the self. As an example, Noon and Lewis (1992) have compared and contrasted a Euro-American definition of appropriate behaviour with a particular Japanese definition (*'Naikan'*) derived from Buddhist ideology. They suggest that within each culture differences in emphasis can be found on the relative importance of the private, public or collective self. In Japan and a number of comparable cultures there is a greater tendency to define the self in a collective sense and thus a greater concern for *collective* responsibility, whereas in the Euro-American case there is a tendency to define the self in a private sense and, therefore, a greater concern with *personal* responsibility. This has implications for the ways in which help can be offered. To offer a form of help, for example, which is directed to strengthening self-concept in terms of the private self may be ineffective for an individual whose self is defined primarily in terms of the collective self, and vice versa.

These differences are particularly relevant to helpers from a western tradition of counselling or psychotherapy, since the aims of such approaches are predicated on the view that the ideal form of self-concept is a strong private self and this is fundamental to coping. For this reason, standard western models of counselling may have limited applicability to someone who holds a cultural belief in collective or public responsibility. The main implication for helpers is that they must avoid the insular assumption that their view of relationships and responsibilities is the only one. Be prepared to learn from those you are endeavouring to help and, once again, be prepared to seek advice from someone or some organization familiar with the culture in question.

These, then, are just a few examples of the diversity of representations of emotional experience and many more can be found. This diversity raises several issues for helpers. Of particular importance is the question of whether the same types of helping response are likely to generalize between different cultures and ethnic groups or whether, instead, each community must have its own unique form of help to reflect its specific needs. In other words, is the general guidance provided in this book relevant to all ethnic and cultural groups?

On the whole, there are enough similarities between the needs of carers from different cultures and ethnic communities to warrant the generalizations made in this book. There seem to be a core of experiences that transcend culture and ethnicity. This core is amenable to the help described here. Around the core, though, there are different layers of norm and convention for each cultural and ethnic group and this may influence specific aspects of help-giving. Despite this, the evidence shows that carers and people cared for from a range of communities do have comparable needs. As helpers we must face the challenge of developing our awareness and sensitivity towards differences in the expression of these needs and recognize that the similarities between the various communities within a society are likely to be greater than the differences. In the paper by Noon and Lewis (1992) described on p. 50, the conclusion was that the goals of helping can be viewed as universal, but the means by which these goals are achieved may vary depending on the specific values of a culture. The route to providing help may differ, but the destination is the same.

Concluding Remarks

This chapter has examined the task of helping and the nature of carers' needs. It is concluded that the levels of need and distress in carers depend upon a variety of factors, the combination of which produces variation between individuals. Accordingly, generalizations about the degree of distress experienced by carers must be moderated in the light of individual differences in the nature of the caring task and the personal, social and statutory resources available for support.

In some cases, the solutions to this distress may be quite straightforward. For instance, if the problem is a lack of information, then the solution is to provide information and enable the carer to identify further sources of information and advice. This has particular relevance to the material burden of caring. Thus material difficulties – finances, housing, aids around the home, methods of managing difficult behaviour – all have potential solutions if you know where to look for relevant information and advice. Provision of help at this level will also alleviate or even pre-empt the development of the emotional burden and its consequences on the emotional wellbeing of the carer.

In some cases, though, the emotional burden may be greater than can easily be helped by information and advice alone. Factors such as the carer's history of coping will determine how easily or with what difficulty he or she deals with the task of caring. Sometimes skills may have become temporarily obscured, and at other times there may be a lack of relevant skills so that the carer needs help to develop them.

The helper is encouraged to use an individually tailored approach to helping. Effective helping depends on a clear identification of the individual carer's specific difficulties, leading to the definition of personally relevant changes that can be made by the carer as his or her capacity to cope is enhanced and facilitated. The question we must always ask is *who* requires *what* help *when*?

Summary

❑ Helping entails a collaborative relationship between helper and carer.

❑ Carers are variable in their needs and so helping must be eclectic.

❑ Carers may not always subscribe to traditional assumptions about the conditions for seeking help.

❑ The difficulties for which carers seek help may not directly be the carer's, but rather those of the person cared for. Therefore, there should be direct help for the carer, for his or her own needs, and indirect help, via the carer, for the needs of the person cared for.

❑ Characteristics of the relationship between carer and person cared for include:

- the gender of the carer and person cared for;
- the quality of the previous relationship between carer and person cared for;
- the nature and severity of disturbance in the person cared for.

❑ The material burden of caring reflects:

- material difficulties such as financial hardship and poor housing;
- practical help with aids around the home and other resources;
- information and advice on practical problems, such as incontinence, behavioural difficulties and general physical care.

❑ The emotional burden of caring includes:

- caring for the dependent other at home;
- lack of support for the carer;
- the carer's poor physical health;
- individual coping styles adopted by carers.

❑ Issues relating to culture and ethnicity involve:

- the needs of carers from different cultural and ethnic groups (what are the similarities and differences?);
- attitudes to seeking and receiving help;
- the communication of distress;
- cultural variation in the means by which help may be provided.

5

Helping: The Basic Skills

The previous chapters have aimed to describe the characteristics of caring, the special features of the carer's task that distinguish carers as a population from others seeking help, the specific needs reported by carers and the basis for coping or not coping. A series of questions follow. How can helpers respond to the needs identified by carers and facilitate coping? What can be said about the kinds of help that carers need? What forms can that help take? Who can provide the help? As these questions are addressed, it will again become apparent that in the same way that carers' needs are various, so must the response be varied to meet those needs.

The approach taken in this book is that the task of helping entails a collaborative relationship with the carer, as a means by which needs can be first identified and then strategies found to meet them. Because of the variability within and between carers in their respective needs, the provision of help must be eclectic. Accordingly, the task of helping requires flexibility to allow the variety of carers' needs to be addressed. This flexibility is not just a matter of being able to use different approaches as a helper; it is also a reflection of the characteristics that distinguish carers from other client groups seeking help. I will attempt to map out and provide a rationale for this eclecticism.

There are two aspects to the helping task. One is a general set of basic skills that underpin all forms of helping; the other is a set of specific strategies for delivering those skills. In this chapter we will look at the general helping skills required by all helpers if they are to provide useful and effective help for carers. In the next chapter, specific strategies will be described. The overriding goal for helpers is to enable carers *to help themselves* and, in so doing, to care more effectively for the other(s) as well as themselves.

The Helping Relationship

The relationship between the carer and the helper provides the foundation of the skills I will describe in this chapter. The helping relationship has been defined by Rogers (1961) as having three principal attributes: empathy, warmth and genuineness.

Empathy is perhaps the most important factor in the helping relationship. Empathy is the quality of being able to relate to the other's distress and show understanding. It is very important that this is not just superficial ('Oh, don't worry dear, I understand exactly what it is like') but a real attempt to see the world as though through the other's eyes and to take the carer's perspective. In effect, as the helper you must ask yourself, 'What is it like to be this carer, to be faced with these demands on a daily basis, to have experienced these changes in one's life?' Of course, true empathy is difficult to achieve, but the struggle to understand the other is the very process which enables a helper to cast a new light on the carer's difficulties and to open up the possibility of new ways of coping. Empathy can be taken to advanced stages in which, as well as being able to understand, as though from the carer's own perspective, the helper attempts to move beyond it and see the carer's difficulties from a number of different perspectives. These different points of view can then be reflected back to the carer and, hopefully, enable him or her to consider new strategies for coping.

Warmth entails the carer perceiving the helper as emotionally warm or approachable. This means being non-judgemental as a helper; not allowing your preconceptions to colour your attitude to the difficulties experienced by the other; treating the carer with respect.

Genuineness refers to the ability of the helper to demonstrate honesty and sincerity. The helper is not expected merely to conform, but to establish a genuine relationship in which differences as well as similarities of view can be discussed openly. Although sometimes challenging, this is really another way of showing respect and of emphasizing the collaborative nature of the helping enterprise.

In effect, the helper using all these principles is saying:

I am not an expert who will solve your problems for you. We know that the difficulties you are facing are too complex for simplistic solutions. And I am not here to judge you. I will do my best to understand your dilemmas without criticism or blame, but if I see things differently I will tell you and leave you to decide which view is most productive. If you agree to work with me then I will put my skills at your disposal and collaborate with you to see whether it is possible for you to deal with the difficulties you experience in a better way.

We are usually taught not to judge by appearances. However, for helpers, appearance – how the helper is perceived – can be an important precondition for establishing a helping relationship (Strong, 1968). In my own experience of working with older adults, I discovered soon after qualifying as a clinical psychologist that my interventions had a different effect when I dressed smartly than when I dressed casually. This is not just a matter of encouraging conventionality in helpers. Rather it is a matter of recognizing and showing respect for the other's values. The generation of older people with whom I was working at that time had an established set of expectations about the formality of our relationship. As a private individual I might have chosen to ignore or even challenge these, but I judged that this would undermine any attempt on my part to offer help. At the beginning of the helping relationship in particular, it was important not to allow my own rules of convention to create an obstacle to those who might seek help.

It is important to stress, though, that establishing a helping relationship does *not* entail the helper being uncritically compliant with every thought or behaviour the carer may express. As helpers, we have to make a beginning. Once a relationship has been established there will be a foundation on which challenges may be made if necessary. However, to challenge another person's values in the earliest stages of helping would be counterproductive.

These characteristics in the helper are the foundation of successful helping. Indeed, if they are not present, the enterprise of helping is likely to fail. The helping relationship provides a foundation on which the helper can then successfully undertake the task of helping. The essential point is that a positive relationship needs to be established before any help can be provided. Furthermore, positive relationships do not always happen spontaneously; sometimes they have to be fostered. The helping skills described next are directed towards this task.

The skills that underpin the helping relationship are generically termed *counselling skills*. Counselling skills are, of course, the basis of formal counselling. However, as they are described in this book they also describe the skills used by all helpers (nurses, social workers, physiotherapists, occupational therapists, doctors, paramedical staff) interacting with patients or clients. In fact, it is impossible not to use counselling skills, since they are the basis of any helping relationship. The question is not whether they are used, but how well. As I mentioned at the beginning of this book, in order to avoid confusion, I will henceforth refer to counselling skills as *helping skills*. Every health-care worker inevitably uses (well or badly) helping skills when he or she works in some capacity with a patient or client. The success of the interaction that takes place depends on the degree of skill possessed by the helper. This is clearly illustrated by two examples from the medical literature.

The first comes from Freund *et al.* (1971). They were investigating the effects of a weight-reducing drug. They discovered that different physicians produced different results, even when they were using exactly the same medication. Their conclusions are worth quoting at length (p. 177):

The eight physicians participating in the study were randomly selected from a resident population. They were then 'conditioned' to relate to the patients in a predetermined manner. Nevertheless, even under these standardised conditions, the first week data demonstrated that the participating physicians were not uniformly capable of producing similar therapeutic results. This supports the long-held belief that physicians differ in the 'art of medicine' and in the quality of 'bedside manner'.... If either Doctor C or Doctor D had been the sole investigator, ... entirely different conclusions might have been reached as to the effectiveness of the test drug. Apart from the action of the drug and the patient's age, sex, education and social status, the effect of the physician's personality and the manner in which he related to the patients had a significant effect on therapeutic outcome.

Similar conclusions can be drawn from other medical procedures. In the realm of surgery, for instance, the attitude of the surgeon can have a profound effect on outcome. Benson and McCallie (1979) provide a dramatic example of this with a procedure known as internal mammary ligation. This procedure was originally used in cardiac surgery as an active treatment for angina and involves re-routing the blood flow by tying one of the arteries. Internal mammary ligation was enthusiastically promoted as the treatment of choice for angina and a theoretical rationale was presented in terms of improvements in the circulation of blood. Numerous operations were performed with a high rate of apparent success: '38 per cent found complete relief, and 65 to 75 per cent showed considerable improvement' (p. 1426). Later, however, more sceptical investigators performed the operation with a placebo control in which anaesthetic was given and an incision in the chest wall was made but without the ligation. This, it transpired, produced the same outcome. The conclusion was that the efficacy of internal mammary ligation derives from the enthusiasm of the doctors rather than the objective consequences of the operation.

What do these examples demonstrate? They show that any helping enterprise, even the administration of a drug or the practice of surgery, can be influenced by the relationship between helper and patient or client. The factors that influence this relationship have been of interest to psychologists and psychotherapists for many years. The term commonly used to describe this helping relationship is the *therapeutic alliance* (e.g. Luborsky *et al.*, 1988).

Horvath *et al.* (1993) examined a number of studies of psychotherapy and identified the ingredients of a successful therapeutic alliance. They are:

1. 'The client's perception of the relevance and potency of the intervention offered.'
2. 'The client's agreement with the therapist on reasonable and important expectations of the therapy in the short and medium term.'
3. 'A cognitive and affective component, influenced by the client's ability to forge a personal bond with the therapist and the therapist's ability to present himself or herself as a caring, sensitive and sympathetic, helping figure' (quoted in Roth and Fonagy, 1996, p. 351).

Although Horvath *et al.* were interested in the common ingredients of successful psychotherapy, exactly the same factors have been identified in counselling, and Noon (1998) has suggested they also account for the efficacy of a wide range of medical treatments. While formal counselling and psychotherapy approaches address the therapeutic alliance explicitly, other forms of helping, including the helping skills described in this book, also depend on the presence of these characteristics.

It must be recognized, then, that the quality of the *relationship* between helper and, in this case, carer is fundamental to the success of helping. The importance of this is not just restricted to formal counselling or psychological therapy, but is also apparent in everyday helping interactions. Even the standard six-minute appointment with a physician or a brief conversation with an occupational therapist at a day centre will vary in effectiveness to the extent that the relationship factors are taken into account.

As described earlier, the components of this relationship include qualities in the helper which enable the carer to establish trust, respect and confidence. One of the problems of modern health care is that the idea of a helper forming a relationship with a client of any kind – including carers – is almost alien to some staff and managers. For instance, certain health-care workers feel that there should be a distance between clinical staff and users of the service because, it is suggested, this protects the staff from uncontainable demands. The assumption, or fear, is that, faced with the unrestricted demands of those being helped, levels of anxiety among staff would soar and they would be unable to cope.

In a well known study of this attitude, Menzies-Lyth (1988) interpreted patterns of organization of staff duties as defences against anxiety. Thus, for example, a task-centred distribution of work, in which a nurse performs a number of specific tasks for a large number of patients, but has no time to perform the full range of necessary tasks for any single patient, prevents the formation of relationships. Each patient experiences the totality of his or her needs as the province of several nurses. While receiving adequate material care, there is a fragmentation of personal relationships and, consequently, of emotional care.

The same principle can be extended to other aspects of health care. For example, patients who receive treatment for limb problems, or back problems, or neck problems or, indeed, problems with any bit of their body, are apt to be treated as a piece of anatomy, in which the functioning of one part is treated as though it were independent of the whole person. Dissatisfaction with this philosophy is a partial explanation of renewed interest in holistic approaches, where such distinctions are avoided.

Egan (1990) also identifies the attributes he considers fundamental to the helping relationship. They encompass those just described but, in addition, he includes two more which in my view are of vital importance. One is *client self-responsibility* and the other is *pragmatism*. The first of these attributes is best described by a direct quote (p. 72): 'Client self-responsibility is a core value of the helping process. It is assumed that, within limits, women and men are capable of making choices and, to some degree, controlling their destinies.'

Helpers must view those offered help as potentially able to regain full responsibility for their lives, even if they have temporarily lost control. If individual carers have no confidence in their self-worth, then they are unlikely to believe they can control their destiny. This, in turn, underlies the failure to cope. The process of helping will often begin by identifying this lack: the feeling of helplessness, hopelessness, or powerlessness. The aim is to provide the opportunities for self-worth, and thus coping, to be restored.

The second category of attributes described by Egan consists of a number of sub-categories, and these are discussed under separate sub-headings in the following section.

Pragmatism

Pragmatism is the ability of the helper to take a practical stance in relation to the carer's needs – the ability to be flexible, to avoid being governed by dogma. The full meaning of the term is encompassed in the following sub-headings.

Keep the client's agenda in focus

Every helper has his or her own agenda when offering help. We as helpers all possess a model of what it is to cope, or to care effectively. The starting point in helping is often an imbalance in power between the helper and the person seeking help. Accordingly, it is easy, as a helper, to make assumptions about what the carer may want or need and, in doing so, to miss the point completely. As a helper, you cannot relinquish your own agenda entirely, but you must try your hardest not to let it eclipse your capacity to listen to the carer. The basic rule is *do not let your own agenda take over*.

Carer (angrily): I need some information. *Nobody seems to want to tell me anything. I have been ignored by the doctor and all the nurses are so busy, but I need someone to talk to me and tell me what is happening.*
Helper: You must be finding it very hard to come to terms with your wife's illness.
Carer (even more angrily): Of course I'm finding it bloody hard, because no one will tell me anything!

This example illustrates a common error found in the work of inexperienced professionals, and sometimes in that of experienced professionals too! The fault lies in allowing the helper's agenda, which, in this case, is about the underlying dynamics of the carer's anger, to intrude into the current interchange. Even if the carer is over-reacting, and even if this over-reaction is indicative of some deeper psychological complexity, the point is that the helper's comments are mis-timed. The request for information is quite legitimate and must be dealt with at face value. If the anger persists beyond this and if the helper is able to have some continuity in his or her meetings with the carer, then it might be possible reasonably to enquire whether the carer finds anger to be a more general problem. If so, then this could be explored immediately, or the carer could be offered the option of seeking specialist help (e.g. from a clinical psychologist or accredited counsellor) if the problem is beyond the helper's competence.

What, then, could the helper have said in response to the carer's opening comments?

Carer (angrily): I need some information. *Nobody seems to want to tell me anything. I have been ignored by the doctor and all the nurses are so busy, but I need someone to talk to me and tell me what is happening.*
Helper: Okay, Mr Jones, let us begin by finding out exactly what you do know and then we can see what further information you need. Have you been told anything at all about Mrs Jones' illness?

Avoid generating resistance

Do not get into a battle with the carer. The aim is to encourage the carer first to recognize the need for help and then to accept that help. If the carer feels threatened or browbeaten by the

helper, then the help tendered may, instead, be taken as inter-
ference, or criticism or judgement or arrogance.

Consider another interchange, overheard on a hospital ward:

*Helper: You know you really should see our psychologist. He is here
to help people just like you.*
*Mrs Smith (irritably): I don't need a psychologist. What are you
trying to say, I'm crazy?*
*Helper: No, of course not. But you are obviously having difficulty
in coping.*
*Mrs Smith: Well so would you if you had to deal with what I have
to deal with.*
Helper: Look Mrs Smith, I am trying to help for heaven's sake!

If you, as a helper, believe you can clearly see the problem and a
potential solution, but this is not consistent with the way the
carer sees it, there will be little profit in expressing your view
directly if it leads only to obstinacy and conflict between the
two of you. The whole point of helping is to introduce different
perspectives so that the carer's views will be expanded and
developed in order for change to occur.

The fundamental issue, though, is how this is done. Any act
or comment that signals to the carer that the helper thinks he or
she knows better is likely to generate resistance in the carer.
Nobody enjoys being told they are not coping and that someone
else can see through them. Any differences in perspective must
be introduced gently and gradually in a way that does not
alienate the carer. In this way, the carer is invited to consider
alternatives and make his or her own choice about the best
option. How, then, might the above interchange have taken
place if these considerations had been observed?

*Helper: I know how difficult it can be dealing with all of this. Do
you have any help or support, anyone to talk to?*
Mrs Smith: Oh, I will cope.
*Helper: Well, I am sure you will do your best and your best may
well be good enough. I just want you to know that if you do have
difficulties there are people here who will try to help you find your
way around some of the problems you may encounter. Please bear
that in mind and let us know if you would like to discuss it again.*
Mrs Smith: Thank you. I will think about it.

Maintain a real-life focus and develop a bias towards action

This means that you should identify goals and targets for the carer that will enhance coping on a day-to-day basis. Having identified goals and targets, act: put the theory into practice. The aim is to ensure that the helping process has practical consequences. There is little point in developing a complex and sophisticated theoretical understanding of the carer's difficulties if this does not have any practical consequences in terms of the carer's behaviour. Remember the definition of helping offered at the beginning of this chapter. The task consists of *enabling carers to help themselves and, in so doing, to care more effectively for the other(s) as well as themselves.*

Helper: And so, Mr Hindley, as I have explained already, there is a link between stress, the mind and the end organs of your autonomic nervous system, such that your tendency catastrophically to mis-interpret physical symptoms in Mrs Hindley as signs of disease actually exacerbates your own physical sensations and makes you feel ill!
Mr Hindley: Oh, really? How fascinating! Got any advice, then?

The moral of the story? Do not try to blind the patient or client with science. The reasons underlying the problem are one thing, but technical explanations should be offered only as a means of enhancing an explanation that is meaningful to the carer, otherwise the technical explanation is mere jargon. Any technical account needs to be accompanied by practical advice and guidance.

Stay flexible

There is no point in sticking to formulae if they do not produce the results. If a theory of helping states, for instance, 'be non-directive', or 'giving advice is not the same as counselling', then by all means start with these considerations in mind. However, if it becomes clear that advice would be useful and that some sort of structure would facilitate desired change, then you have to be flexible enough to acknowledge that there is more than one theory of helping and be prepared to adopt a different stance. In brief, 'do whatever is ethical and works' (Egan, 1990).

How, then, will you know whether or not the approach you have been taking is working? Ask yourself: What are the goals of my helping? Has anything been achieved by the help I have provided? Is there a sense, for either of us, of being stuck, or of not making progress? If you have lost sight of the goals, or if there is a sense of little having been achieved and a feeling of stagnation, then it is worth reconsidering the approach you have been taking. It is particularly helpful to seek advice from an experienced counsellor or clinical psychologist in such cases.

Do only what is necessary

Do not get carried away with the task of helping. It is, in fact, very rewarding to see one's helping efforts producing good results. The relationship that develops between helper and carer can be strong, rewarding and seductive, in the sense that it can become the reason for continuing to offer help beyond the point that was originally identified as the goal. Be clear about your aims and review these periodically during your meetings with the carer. When they have been achieved, review with the carer whether any further goals have become apparent. If not, identify an endpoint to your involvement and work towards this. In brief, stick to the agenda!

Do not offer helping as a panacea

People who are distressed often have high and sometimes unrealistic expectations of what can be achieved in the process of helping. It is very easy to want to promote optimism and reinforce these expectations. It is also very easy to over-sell yourself. Remember that the aim of helping is to help carers to help themselves, and this means that you are the facilitator but not the agent of change. Therefore, do not build up unrealistic expectations.

Dealing with the expectations of carers can be particularly difficult for health professionals whose role may, sometimes, entail being the agent of change. For instance, doctors are often expected to effect cures and both they and their patients may reasonably work towards this aim in some circumstances. The helping role as defined in this book is different. The wish for a cure in the task of caring is not realistic. The only realistic option for the majority of problems described in this book is better coping skills to deal with the continuing stresses. It is not surprising, however, if you, as a professional who sometimes undertakes the task of looking for a cure, then find it difficult to switch in and out of roles and become a helper who has no cure to offer. Indeed, some professionals find the sense of impotence this creates intolerable. It may be difficult both for you and for the person seeking help, whose expectations may relate to your usual professional role rather than the role of a helper as it is defined in this book. This dilemma, which applies to both professionals and the recipients of help, is further discussed in Noon (1992).

The Foundations of Helping I: Attending and Listening Skills

If a relationship can be established and the carer becomes engaged in the helping process, then there are a number of foundation skills involved in enhancing and facilitating communication. In describing these, it is worth noting the points made earlier in Chapters 2 and 3 relating to the cultural differences in the conventions for many of the skills that will be described below (see also Noon and Lewis, 1992). The helper is advised to be sensitive to the possibility of individual differences, for instance reflecting ethnicity or gender, and look for signs of awkwardness and discomfort in the carer, which may indicate that the helper's approach needs to be re-appraised.

I know of one specialist who, as patients enter his office and sit down, deliberately and very obviously looks at his watch. The effect is dramatic. The patient suddenly speeds up and hastily gabbles his or her message to this busy man, who is obviously so hard pressed for time. Afterwards, patients undoubtedly think of all the things they had meant to say before the anxiety had been induced in them by the specialist's action. He, of course, is indeed a very busy man and uses this deliberate strategy, in his view, 'to get to the heart of things and cut out all the unnecessary verbiage'.

The question is whether the information he elicits really does get to the heart of the matter. Experience shows that most patients want to understand their condition and prognosis. They may legitimately enquire about the cause, likely duration and severity of their condition, and seek advice about prevention of further complications and information about medication. If patients are able to identify the information they need and, perhaps, take with them a list of questions, they may actually require less time in the consultation than if they are not prepared. Being prepared can shorten a consultation because communication can be more direct.

Attending skills

Paying attention is a sign of respect, just as being uninterested is an insult. An averted gaze can imply guilt, anxiety, shame or boredom and is not conducive to the development of trust. Equally, a hard stare can be threatening. Observe the way friends convey their friendship by their gaze and facial expressions. The message you, as a helper, need to convey is: 'You have my undivided attention; I am here to try to understand what you wish to tell me.' Of course, there is a real dilemma for helpers who do actually have only a short time to give and who have to see a large number of clients or patients during a fixed period of time. However, even in these circumstances, it is likely that ten minutes spent with a carer who believes you are interested will produce more relevant information than ten minutes spent with someone impaired by anxiety induced by the helper's unsympathetic attitude.

Posture and proximity

Your posture and proximity are important as a means of signalling to the carer your concern and respect for his or her distress. Leaning towards the carer can convey interest. Sitting squarely facing the carer is a sign of attention. The distance between you can be critical: too near induces discomfort, too far creates psychological as well as physical distance. You will need to experiment with these variables until you find, by trial and error, what suits you and the people you are seeking to help.

Facial expression and gesture

Think about conversations you have with others. Notice the way you both watch each other's face for signs of mood, surprise, outrage, pleasure. When you are with a carer be aware that he or she too will be reading your face in the same way and so it is important that your facial expression is congruent with the task you are trying to achieve in working with the carer.

Similarly, gesticulation and general bodily movement signal a host of meanings: anxious wringing of hands, impatient tapping of fingers, tenseness in the shoulders, scratching your head. Think about the ways your body reflects your state of mind. Think also about how your body sometimes, unconsciously, betrays an attitude that is inconsistent with the message you want to signal. Becoming familiar with these signals will aid you in understanding the carer's non-verbal communications and will also enable you to be more conscious of the non-verbal signals you convey to the carer.

Paralinguistic cues

Voice loudness, pitch, timbre, intonation, speed of talking, pausing and fluency are all a reflection of the relationship between speakers, and the ability to recognize the message behind these cues is a sign of the honesty or genuineness which is a prerequisite for helping. If the person you are helping is sad and softly spoken and you respond with fast, loud speech, then the mood of the dialogue is lost: you have not achieved congruence. The task is first to recognize and then to work alongside the mood of the carer. There will be times when working alongside may mean adopting a different set of paralinguistic behaviours. For example, if the carer is anxious, then it would be inappropriate to respond with paralinguistic signals of your own anxiety. Sometimes you may want to slow things down, to create space by reducing the pace of the interaction. Get used to reading the signs and let these guide your response.

Paralinguistic cues are particularly valuable in enabling the helper to distinguish any discrepancies between what the carer says and what he or she really feels. This is an example of advanced empathy, in which the helper can look beyond the ostensible message and provide a different perspective for the carer. For instance, the carer who says, 'No, really, I am coping fine,' with tears in his or her eyes, a stooping posture and general demeanour of sadness, is betraying his or her real feelings, despite any words to the contrary. It is useful, as a helper, to look for these discrepancies. Sometimes it is appropriate to draw attention to them, in a gentle way: 'Yet I see you have a tear in your eye. I wonder what it is that makes you sad right now?' The effect of the right comment at the right time can be quite dramatic. The carer is likely to feel that here is someone who understands his or her real feelings; someone who is not deceived by appearances; who has communicated that it is all right to be sad, or angry, or anxious, and so on. The carer may then feel released by this: freed from the need to maintain a brave face.

Active listening

Active listening is the ability to draw together all the disparate threads of the communication process and find meaning. The attending and listening skills described are part of the *process* of communication and the helper must develop his or her skills in recognizing and understanding these. In addition, there is the *content* of communication: what is spoken; the words; the message. The helper must hear both the process and the content of communication and look for consistency or discrepancy between them. If there is discrepancy, then this means that what is ostensibly communicated is not what is really believed or felt by the carer. The helper's task is to enable the carer to recognize these contradictions and be able to express what is really meant or felt. The helper must also relate what is communicated to the wider context of the carer's social and personal environment and attempt to use the skills of empathy to understand the carer's perception of things and the extent to which this is consistent with the facts. For instance, if the carer perceives himself or herself as failing in the task of caring, the helper, while understanding these feelings, may wish to question the basis for the carer's belief. What is the evidence? Would an independent observer come to the same conclusions? Are there other interpretations of events?

Active listening is a manifestation of advanced empathy. It is the ability to hear the words that are spoken and to relate these to the non-verbal and paralinguistic cues described to understand the message beneath what is said. For instance, if someone says 'I really like Fred!' in an intonation that is clearly ironical, then we have no difficulty in recognizing that the speaker really does not like Fred at all. The philosopher Paul Grice has provided a nice example of the ways in which meaning can be expressed indirectly. He describes a university lecturer who is asked for a reference for an ex-student applying for an academic post. The lecturer writes: 'Smith is usually punctual and has a good command of English.' And that is all he writes! What would you as the potential employer make of such a reference? It is hardly a glowing testimony. Yet there is nothing actually negative in the reference. It is all done through implication: it is what the reference does *not* say that carries the meaning. The implication is that the referee is not all that impressed with Smith and does not wish to support his application, but does not want to be seen to be saying anything explicitly negative. As a helper you too must get used to seeing the message behind the surface of what is said. What is implied? What is not said, or avoided? Are there incongruities between the words and the gestures, or the facial expressions, and so forth? Does he mean what he says? Does she say what she means?

The Foundations of Helping II: Problem Exploration and Clarification

As communication develops, there will be a need to clarify what is said and ensure that the problems are explored as fully as possible. As will be apparent in the earlier sections, what is communicated may not always be what is truly felt or meant and any discrepancies or confusions need to be identified and resolved. The following skills are directed towards this goal.

Prompting

One of the most difficult aspects of helping is getting started. The carer will sometimes need a prompt to begin. Basic phrases like *'Is there anything you need to know?'* can give the carer an opportunity to start. Open questions, such as this, are usually better than closed questions, such as 'Are you well?' or, 'Is your wife/husband any better these days?', since the latter usually elicit a yes/no response and inhibit further expansion.

Helper: I understand you were asking about what help is available. What are the main difficulties at the moment?

Some carers remain reluctant to acknowledge difficulties, especially in the early stages of contact with a helper. Indeed, the suggestion there might be difficulties can be perceived as a threat or a criticism. Remember that even if carers do have emotional needs stemming from the experience of caring, they may not find it easy to acknowledge these needs and to request or accept help. Indeed, far from seeking help, they may be quite wary of it: 'I suppose you think it's "all in my mind"?', or 'Isn't it only mentally ill people who need helping?', or 'You must think I'm neurotic'. It may help to pre-empt the idea that there are no difficulties by phrasing your question in a way that *normalizes* the idea that difficulties are to be expected:

Helper: Most people find it difficult adapting to the changes you've experienced. What kinds of difficulty are you finding at the moment?

If you can begin to make contact with the carer at these levels then the chances of acknowledging any emotional level of difficulty are increased. The carer, feeling safer, may be able to respond.

Carer: Oh, yes it can be a strain. I try my best to cope, but it isn't easy.

The door is now open to further exploration:

Helper: I'm sure it is a strain. And it must take its toll on you. Carers often find it helps to talk their difficulties over. Do you think it might help to talk about those difficulties a bit more?

Sometimes the response might be something like 'I can't see how it's going to help,' or 'I'm the only one who is going to be able to sort this out,', or 'There must be lots of people with far worse problems than me; I wouldn't want to waste your time.' In such cases the helper will have to explain the rationale of helping – how a different perspective can sometimes allow new insights; how the helper is not going to take over responsibility for finding solutions but may facilitate the carer's own problem-solving skills; how working with the carer at this stage can prevent bigger problems from arising later.

If the carer responds positively and decides that further help is indicated, do not forget the practicalities which are particularly important in helping carers:

Helper: It will take time. Can you find the time to come and talk to me a bit more?' 'What about ... [the person cared for]? Is there someone who can help you out while you come here? ... We might need to meet a few times to discuss this – will that be possible for you?

Having arrived at this stage, you will then be in a position to embark on more detailed helping, involving further exploration and clarification.

Questioning

As helping proceeds, you will have to ask questions from time to time to clarify what is said, or to elicit new information. I have already referred to open and closed questions. Open questions allow carers to elaborate their account of the difficulties for which they seek help. They also avoid a potential danger of closed questions, namely that they may give the impression that the helper is interrogating the carer.

Carer: I can't seem to be bothered with anything. I can't see the point. I have had enough.
Helper: How long have you felt like this?
Carer: For a few months now.
Helper: Were you ever like this before?
Carer: No.
Helper: And is it everything that seems pointless?
Carer: Yes, everything.

The problem in the above excerpt is that the helper, who is using closed questions, is doing a lot of talking but gaining relatively little information. Compare this with the following open question.

Carer: I can't seem to be bothered with anything. I can't see the point. I have had enough.
Helper: What have you had enough of?
Carer: Everything: the caring, the looking after, always having to be there. I feel like a prisoner.
Helper: Can you tell me what that means, to 'feel like a prisoner'?

The carer has been offered an opportunity to speak and now has a chance to articulate exactly what the feeling is and its effects on his or her life and the lives of relevant others.

Questioning, in general, should be used to help the carer elucidate his or her difficulties. The helper's skilful questioning is not just a means of acquiring information, although there is a place for this. More than this, though, questions are an opportunity for the carer to 'think out loud', to put words to experiences and to articulate difficulties. In doing so the carer may see things from a different perspective and reveal new aspects of his or her experience.

Paraphrasing and summarizing

Paraphrasing and summarizing are further examples of empathy. They are a means of showing that you, the helper, have attempted to see the world from the carer's point of view. This serves a dual purpose: it allows the helper to confirm his or her understanding and it allows the carer some feedback and confirmation about the helper's understanding. Paraphrasing can also be linked to summarizing, more briefly, what has been said and presenting it in such a way that it will throw a new light on the problem:

Carer: I really do still love her. There are times when she is just like her old self, except in a more innocent way, a bit like a child. And then, other times, I shout at her because she is behaving like a child. She must get so hurt when I do that and I don't mean to hurt her. But I can't seem to handle that. I get confused myself and keep my feelings in and will spend all day not saying anything to her. It's not because I am angry with her any more. It's just that I don't know what to say.

Helper (paraphrasing): Even though you love her, her behaviour can still frustrate you and this makes you feel guilty.

Carer: Yes, that's right.

Helper (summarizing): So your main concern is that you are worried about the mixed messages that you think you give her and you don't know how to deal with that. You don't know what to say to her that will explain your real feelings?

Challenging what is said

Eliciting information from carers will often be complicated by the fact that their understanding will not always conform to others' understanding of the same events: this, after all, is not unique to carers. These differences in understanding can work in both directions. Sometimes it can be to the apparent disadvantage of the carer, sometimes to his or her apparent benefit. For instance, carers who believe that the care they are giving is inadequate may be profoundly underrating the skill and dedication they put into the task. Similarly, carers who believe they are doing as much as possible may be overestimating their achievements. These discrepancies, in turn, may reflect underlying characteristics, either of the carer or of the relationship between carer and the person cared for.

In addition, we all make assumptions about what others think or predictions about how they will behave. Sometimes these assumptions may not be valid and will benefit from being challenged. In challenging the carer, however, the helper is not trying to demonstrate that he or she is right and the carer wrong. Indeed, the most effective challenges occur when the carer is invited by the helper to challenge his or her own beliefs. The aim is to take another look at things and check if the inferences and assumptions that have already been made are the best or the only ones possible. This, though, must be undertaken strategically. A challenge need not be an interrogation. Indeed, a head-on challenge may fail whereas an indirect challenge may succeed.

One of the most effective means of challenging the other's assumptions is to ask for clarification, or to make a tentative enquiry or suggestion. The person is invited to articulate the underlying belief and check if it is founded on any real evidence. If it is not, then a different belief may be warranted and this may prove more adaptive and helpful for all concerned. By challenging in this way, the helper is demonstrating genuineness and empathy, honesty and understanding. The following case example illustrates these points.

Case example: looking beneath the surface of what is said

Geoffrey was very isolated because of Peter's illness: Peter was HIV positive. Since Peter's illness their physician had come to know them both as regular patients and had built up a good relationship with both. Geoffrey was depressed and had sought help from his physician (the helper).

Helper: Did you find yourself socially isolated before Peter was HIV positive?
Geoffrey: Oh no. We used to have a fantastic social life. Out almost every night we were.
Helper: So what exactly is it that prevents you going out now?

Geoffrey: I couldn't leave Peter at home and go out enjoying myself.
Helper: Why not?
Geoffrey: Well, Peter would hate it.
Helper (challenging Geoffrey's assumptions): Have you asked Peter?
Geoffrey: Well, no, I haven't asked him. But it is obvious isn't it?
Helper (still challenging Geoffrey's assumptions): You know that he doesn't need you to be there all the time, don't you?
Geoffrey: Yes, but that isn't the point. I would feel uncomfortable about going out.
Helper: I am not sure what that means: 'feel uncomfortable'?
Geoffrey: Guilty.
Helper: Do you know what it is you would feel guilty about?
Geoffrey: Well, I just don't think I should have a good time while Peter is having such a bloody awful time. What would he think of me?

The helper continues to challenge Geoffrey's preconceptions about how he predicts Peter would react.

Helper: I don't know: what would he think of you?
Geoffrey: Well, all sorts I am sure.
Helper: But I still don't know exactly what he would think of you.
Geoffrey: Well, he wouldn't like it.
Helper: Do you mean he would resent it?
Geoffrey: Probably.
Helper: But you don't know for certain?
Geoffrey: Well he is sure to, isn't he? What would you expect?

This example of Geoffrey's dilemmas is very typical, in one particular way, of many partner relationships between carers and those cared for. The fact is that the illness of one has had a dramatic effect on the lifestyle of the other. Many carers feel unfulfilled by aspects of their present relationship and deprived of opportunities they once had.

In the above example, the challenges made by the helper have, so far, been relatively gentle and directed towards enabling Geoffrey to examine his own assumptions and predictions about his partner's feelings and behaviour. Of course, Geoffrey may be correct in some of his predictions, but it is rarely the case that all such assumptions are well founded and there is benefit in allowing the fears and expectations which underlie the assumptions to be spelt out.

The helper is also aware that Geoffrey is experiencing feelings, common among a variety of carers, of frustration born out of unfulfilled needs. The dialogue continues as follows:

Helper: Geoffrey, I may be wrong about this, but I wonder if you are partly thinking that Peter's fears and suspicions may not be groundless. When you said you would feel guilty about having a good time, are you afraid that perhaps you would? Do you think there is a chance you might enjoy yourself in a way that Peter would resent? Is that possible?

This is an example of advanced empathy, to which I have referred earlier. The helper has not only demonstrated that she can understand Geoffrey's difficulties, she has also moved beyond Geoffrey's perspective and suggested a deeper understanding. In addition, she has done this in a way that respects Geoffrey's difficulties and dilemmas. It would be possible to say the same thing in a way that implies criticism and induces guilt. However, the helper was deliberately very *tentative* in the way she expressed her view. This is a means of inviting the carer to consider different possibilities, without being confrontational or judgemental. In doing this the helper is enabling Geoffrey to recognize feelings that were latent, unexpressed. If the helper's comments had conveyed criticism, then Geoffrey may have become defensive and denied his feelings. In contrast to this, because the helper was non-judgemental, Geoffrey was able to acknowledge that he did experience the feelings of frustration alluded to by the helper. He did sometimes wish he could have a more fulfilling relationship with someone else: more like the relationship he used to have with Peter. But he is also committed to Peter and so the options are restricted.

The helper's aim is to allow Geoffrey first of all to acknowledge these feelings and see them as understandable. He may also, then, be able to recognize, for example, that his frustration engenders further feelings towards Peter of resentment and anger, as well as guilt. It is possible, and quite common, that these latent feelings of anger and resentment may show themselves indirectly in behaviour towards Peter: getting annoyed with him for trivial reasons; being impatient; being cold and distant. Alternatively, the dormant feelings of anger and resentment may be self-directed and expressed as self-loathing and guilt. The point is that many of these apparently inexplicable feelings, which may have developed over time and have led to a state of depression or chronic distress, can be related to a basic dilemma such as has been described above. Bringing feelings out into the open may be painful at first, but leaving them dormant can be much more painful. Ultimately, the frustration cannot be removed, but what can be removed are the apparently inexplicable feelings and behaviour engendered by that frustration.

Concluding Remarks

These, then are the basic skills that provide a foundation for effective helping; the means by which the task of helping may take place. Every such task has both a general set of basic skills and a specific strategy for the delivery of those skills. These are different facets of the total enterprise. The basic skills described are a set of directions which specify how to carry out a task successfully. But we need more than this – we need a strategy or framework for translating those directions into specific action. In the next chapter I will illustrate how the basic helping skills can be attached to particular strategies for helping. We will move, so to speak, from the general to the particular, with reference to the three strategies mentioned in the previous chapter (see Table 1, p. 37): informational help; support and emotional help; and problem-solving.

Summary

❑ The overriding goal for helpers is to enable carers to help themselves and, in so doing, more effectively to care for the other(s) as well as themselves.

❑ Helping needs to be eclectic, reflecting the variability of carers' needs.

❑ Helping entails a collaborative relationship with the carer as a means by which needs can first be identified and then strategies found to meet them.

❑ The fundamental attributes for relationship building are empathy, warmth, genuineness, client self-responsibility and pragmatism.

❑ The helper is advised to:

- keep the client's agenda in focus;
- avoid generating resistance;
- maintain a real-life focus and develop a bias towards action;
- stay flexible;
- do only what is necessary;
- not offer helping as a panacea.

❑ Attending and listening skills are fundamental to establishing and developing the helping relationship and demonstrating empathy, warmth and genuineness.

❑ The helper's whole attention should be directed towards the carer and this is demonstrated by posture and proximity, facial expression and gesture, non-verbal communication and active listening.

❑ Problem exploration and clarification are achieved by the use of prompting, questioning, paraphrasing, summarizing and challenging.

6

Putting It All Together

The aim of the book up to this point has been to establish the foundations for effective helping. I have described the task of caring, the magnitude of the problem, some characteristics of caring and carers' needs, the underlying assumptions, norms and conventions that influence the carer's self-appraisal and how he or she copes with the task of caring. I have presented a model of coping intended to illustrate what goes on 'behind the scenes' in the process of adjusting to the demands of caring; and I have described the basic skills required by the helper to respond to carers' needs.

In this chapter I would like to pull all these threads together and illustrate the application of helping skills to some of the difficulties experienced by carers. As mentioned earlier, this will take the form of a description of:

1. informational help;
2. support and emotional help;
3. problem-solving.

Later in the chapter I will also refer to what I have termed *complex issues*. My aim in doing so is to provide the reader with a variety of examples, ranging from everyday cases which they are likely to meet regularly, to examples of more complex problems they may encounter at the boundary, so to speak, of their helping skills. This will raise the question of whether to seek specialist help, and I hope the examples will stimulate the reader to consider his or her own position in relation to all the issues raised.

It is worth saying as a preliminary, though, that many of the coping strategies adopted by carers that will be described as potentially problematical are, in fact, ambiguous in terms of their effectiveness: sometimes they work, sometimes they do not. In general it appears that some strategies that may be effective in the short term can become ineffective in the longer term. Take the example of whether or not it is helpful to seek and acquire full information about an illness. It would appear that if an individual is undergoing short-term investigative medical procedures, information can increase distress. However, if the individual has a long-term, chronic condition then information can decrease distress. Steptoe (1991) suggests that in the former case information may increase unnecessary worry about the significance of minor symptoms, while in the latter case information allows more appropriate strategies for self-care to be developed. In what follows, therefore, the point to consider is that while general guidelines will be offered, they should not be considered absolute. I will return to this point when discussing denial.

Informational Help

Informational help is the responsibility of all professionals involved in each aspect of the individual's treatment and care, from the initial physician consultation, through the various specialist treatments, to the aftercare provided in the hospital, home, or hospice. It is the responsibility of all helpers to check what information the person cared for and his or her carer(s) may have or may require at a given time and to provide full information where necessary. Of course, the best helpers recognize that both the person cared for *and* his or her carer(s) need access to information. Unfortunately, though, the carer is sometimes neglected, or approached as an afterthought.

In many cases an individual's informational needs are relatively straightforward. The helper can begin by establishing the carer's current level of knowledge and understanding. This can be achieved by asking carers what they already know and if they have any questions or comments about what they have been told: 'What do you need to know? What would be helpful at the moment?' or, 'Do you have any questions about your partner's (or child's or parent's) condition (or treatment or prognosis)? Have you asked the specialist (or nurse or psychologist) about this?'

If there are gaps in the carer's knowledge or understanding, the helper must then provide information, or at least direct the carer to where information or advice can be found: 'I am not sure I can answer all of your questions, but let us see: what was it you were unsure about?' or, 'Do you know about the organizations that provide information about your partner's (or child's or parent's) condition?', 'Have you contacted the carers' centre?'

Bearing in mind, though, that carers will often be in a state of distress and apprehensiveness, the helper must also check that the information that has been provided has been fully understood: 'Now, let us go over this again and make certain that everything is clear,' or, 'Would you like me to go over that again?'

Another example of good practice in this respect is provided by some medical specialists who, when imparting important diagnostic or prognostic information to patients and their relatives, provide a tape recording of the consultation. The individuals, who are often in a state of some anxiety during the consultation, can then play back the tape later and remind themselves of exactly what was said and also think about anything that is not clear and ask questions at a later date (Hogbin and Fallowfield, 1989).

If the carer recognizes a need for help and requests information, the task is relatively straightforward insofar as the carer has comparable needs to other populations seeking help. Often, though, there may be no explicit request for help from the carer. How does the helper assess the carer's needs in such circumstances? Bear in mind the experience of the organization described earlier which misjudged the ability and willingness of carers to make time for their own needs. Partly this may be a practical issue of finding the time. Partly it might be that the offer of help was directed at the wrong level.

As I mentioned earlier, one way of viewing the task of providing advice and information is in terms of *empowerment*. Unfortunately, it is sometimes the case that the large institutions we have created to provide care are experienced as impersonal and bureaucratic: 'Every time we go there, there's another doctor we've never met before. You have to go over and over the same story. And whenever we get to see the specialist she's always so busy. I don't like to bother her with all our questions.' This, in combination with the experience of illness or disability in someone close, can create the effect in the carer of disempowerment: no choice, no control, impotence. The helper can differ from these experiences by *empowering* the carer with information, advice and guidance. In doing so, the helper will also be using one of the core relationship skills by demonstrating respect for the carer.

Establishing contact with the carer in this way will have the effect of empowering the carer and, in addition, will demonstrate that you are a potential helper. You will then be in a better position to address, if necessary, any further aspects of the carer's needs, such as his or her emotional or problem-solving needs. Take it in stages.

It is important to note, though, that there are limits on the impact of advice and information on carers' distress. For example, Graham *et al.* (1997) found that information provided to carers of people with dementia reduced levels of depression, although not levels of anxiety. This suggests that after being given relevant information, the carers may have felt more in control of their task of caring, but this did not obviate the intrinsic difficulties of caring, which remained stressful. Nevertheless, the degree of *distress* was diminished and this will have helped to reduce their overall emotional burden.

A similar point is made by Sutcliffe and Larner (1988). They distinguish between help in the form of information and advice, on the one hand, and emotional support, on the other. They found that only the latter decreased what I have termed the emotional burden among carers. Information and advice, then, may have a preventative effect and pre-empt the development of emotional problems or they can have an ameliorative effect by reducing the overall extent of emotional problems (as demonstrated by Ballard and Sham, 1997). However, there is a point at which the degree of emotional distress becomes so great that information and advice *alone* are insufficient to ameliorate the difficulties. At this point a different kind of help is required and in the next section we will look more closely at how this may be provided. Nevertheless, information and advice, while limited in their capacity to remove emotional distress once it has become established, can still contribute to a reduction in the *onset* of problematical stress in carers, especially if provided at an earlier stage in the process, before the emotional difficulties have become unmanageable.

It is helpful to think of the distinctions between informational help and emotional help as representing a progression, in the sense that dealing with the former may open up the possibility of dealing with the latter. This is by no means to suggest that informational help is less important or more superficial. The apposite and timely use of basic helping skills serves a very important function and can pre-empt problems of the kind that will require more extensive helping later on. The point here is that for this particular client group there is a question of tactics: how best to provide the opportunity for all the carer's needs to be addressed. If the informational needs of the carer can be addressed, then this also may open up the opportunity for the carer to talk about more emotional issues.

Support and Emotional Help

Emotional support can in some instances be a general task and in others may be the task of a trained counsellor or psychological therapist. As a general task it will involve the basic helping skills described earlier, which are intrinsic to all helping professionals. The aim is to facilitate individuals in the process of acknowledging and then talking honestly about their emotions in relation to the illness or disability of the person cared for and its effect on themselves and others. For carers in particular there is often a heightened sense of guilt about acknowledging their own needs, rather than the ill person's. Thus great relief can be derived by the carer from the recognition that his or her feelings are legitimate and understandable and are not a sign of selfishness and insensitivity. Much can be achieved by the process of what used to be called 'ventilation': that is to say, the free expression of thoughts and feelings about what is happening without being judged. A sensitive helper, by facilitating this process, may pre-empt more serious problems which sometimes build up when difficult thoughts and feelings are inhibited.

Helper: You must find it difficult having to look after your husband all the time. How do you cope with the pressure?
Carer: Oh, me? Goodness my problems are nothing. It's poor Jack who has the problems.
Helper: Yes, I know. But it still can't be easy for you.
Carer: Well I do sometimes wish I could have some time off. You know I've forgotten what it's like to go out for pleasure. I've lost most of my friends. Just one or two good friends who keep in touch. But I can't even find time to contact them. They must think I'm awful, ignoring them like that. If there is a bit of time I'm too exhausted even to make a phone call. Oh, listen to me. You must think 'What's she going on about, it's her husband we should be talking about'.

Helper: No, I'm not thinking that. A lot of the relatives I meet say what you've said. They all find it an incredible strain but feel guilty when they say so.
Carer: Really?

In this example, the ground is now laid to enable the carer to express her needs more fully. She may be interested in the possibility of respite, or there may be an organization that can help her with advice and information. The helper has *normalized* the carer's experience by informing her that it is, in fact, common among other carers. This permits the carer to relinquish some of the guilt she may have been feeling and also allows the possibility of the carer taking pre-emptive action by accepting further help, which may prevent more serious difficulties arising later on.

Social isolation, respite and support

One of the main contributions to the emotional burden faced by carers is the social isolation that the caring role entails. The response to this would, therefore, appear to be some form of support aimed at reducing social isolation. However, not all types of support are equally effective. For instance, while Levin *et al.* (1989) found stress among carers could be alleviated by the support provided by community-based services, Gilleard *et al.* (1984a,b) found contradictory results. One clue to this discrepancy comes from a study by Gilhooly (1984), who made a distinction between community services that did and did not increase carers' psychological wellbeing: home helps and community nursing did; meals-on-wheels and day hospitals did not. Gilhooly also found that dissatisfaction with help received was associated with decreased morale and poorer mental health.

It is worth considering these findings in detail. The point is that the help that is experienced as supportive by carers does not decrease morale. For some reason, in the studies above, meals-on-wheels and day hospitals were not helpful, and it must be concluded that their effects on carers' morale were negative. This is not to say that all day hospitals or all meals-on-wheels services will inevitably have this effect. In particular cases, though, a service may have this effect and helpers must ask why. Is it possible to predict whether our help is likely to have a positive or negative effect on morale?

The answer is to be found in understanding the basis of positive or negative morale. A carer's morale is a reflection of how well he or she is coping and, as has been discussed in an earlier chapter, this is a result of self-appraisal. When any form of help is offered it provides feedback to the carer about how well she or he is succeeding, or not, in the task of caring. Indeed, sometimes an offer of ostensible help may appear to the carer to be a sign of failure: 'Has it come to this? Can't I even manage the cooking now?'

Another example is found in respite care. For some carers the need for respite amounts to a sign that they can no longer cope without external help and this feels like failure. We, as helpers, must, therefore, recognize that it is possible to offer help in ways that can either boost or undermine the carer's morale. If, for example, the help offered is perceived by the carer as a sign of failing to cope, then it may, in turn, be interpreted as implicit criticism. If, on the other hand, help is offered in a way that *affirms* the carer's efforts, then it is more likely to bolster his or her sense of coping. It is only the latter form of help that is truly supportive of the carer. This difference may depend on a number of factors, ranging from material characteristics of the environment to the attitude of the staff. Some day hospitals, for example, are run-down, rather depressing places: impoverished, gloomy; they seem to exude the feeling of desperation. Others offer light, airy, attractive environments which are pleasant to be in. However, even the most materially impoverished environment can be welcoming if the people who work in it are positive about themselves and what they have to offer.

I must stress, though, that the perception of the carer is not always an accurate reflection of the intentions of individual helpers or helping organizations. An organization offering respite and the staff working in it may all be striving hard to present their service as truly supportive. Carers, though, are often under great stress and some may, therefore, be vulnerable to comments or behaviour that can be interpreted as conveying implicit criticism. It is this vulnerability which can colour a carer's perception of the help offered. This emphasizes the need for helpers to ensure that they are using helping skills effectively, in the ways described in earlier chapters. If the carer feels listened to and understood and is shown the respect which is inherent in good communication skills, then she or he is less likely to feel undermined or devalued by the offer of help.

Respite is a valuable resource for all of us. It is 'time-out': an escape from the pressures of perpetual responsibilities. It is a time to sit on the sidelines and recover strength. For most of us who are not carers it is a normal part of the routine of our lives. For instance, work may be demanding, but we have interests outside of work to provide a balance. We may have families, hobbies, holidays and *time*, all of which provide a break from the most arduous and demanding aspects of our lives. This variety is important.

What happens to a person who lacks these balances in his or her life? One possibility is the well known phenomenon of *burnout*. Burnout (Table 2) is what happens when the demands become relentless; when there is seemingly no escape and all our resources are used up. Burnout is the term used to describe the failure to cope with stress to an extent that leads to chronic incapacity to cope. It manifests as emotional exhaustion, depersonalization, low productivity and feelings of low achievement. We all need occasional respite and carers need this more than most. As was illustrated in the previous chapter, carers have enormous demands on their resources. The very task of caring makes impossible the kinds of balance in life that most of us take for granted.

As I have already mentioned, however, a problem for some carers is that respite can seem like an abdication of responsibility: 'He is my husband, how can I leave him for strangers to look

Table 2 The symptoms of burnout

Physical symptoms	Personal symptoms	Behavioural symptoms
Fatigue	Depression	Irritability
Insomnia	Anxiety	Cynicism
Headache	Obsessionality	Defensiveness
Backache	Feeling indispensable	Fault-finding in others
Gastro-intestinal symptoms	Restlessness	Alcohol dependency
Weight gain/loss	Tendency to rationalize	Drug dependency
Shortness of breath	Stagnation	Inability to enjoy others' success
Lingering cold	Boredom	

after, even for a few hours?' or, 'She won't like that; she will think I am going to leave her there for ever,' and so forth. In these cases the helper must be able to reassure the carer about the aims of respite: that if carers take some time for themselves, they will be better able to continue to provide care and that respite of some kind may prevent burnout.

To convey this message, one might begin by acknowledging, for instance, the difficulties of the carer's task: 'I do not know how you have managed to keep going so long,' or, 'I know it is difficult the first time. Some carers feel like they are failing, but they come to recognize that any extra help they can get gives them more time and energy to give to the person they care for in the long run,' or, 'This will let you get your strength back: no one can go on alone indefinitely,' or, 'If you look after yourself, you will be able to look after him (or her) better.'

Len Baker had looked after his wife for 11 years. She had been ill for many years, starting with heart disease and then followed periodically by several strokes, the last of which had left her completely helpless. Len had developed a protective, defensive and rather anxious concern for his wife over that time. Many local staff with whom he had occasional involvement found him quite difficult. They would complain of his 'irritability'. For instance, a nurse said: 'You'd think he would be thankful when we call, but he seems so resentful. I don't like to visit, but I know his wife needs our help.' Len's motives, though, were essentially benevolent. He had a real fear that 'someone out there' would decide his wife needed institutional care. And, in his words: 'Where I come from you look after your own.' Each form of help offered by the local services was perceived as both demeaning – a form of charity, and threatening – a step towards institutional care.

Over the years many people had recognized the toll taken on Len by his eternal vigilance. And many times it had been suggested that perhaps he needed some support. Of course, nothing could have made him feel more entrenched in his views than the suggestion that he was not coping. This was perceived as a criticism and another form of threat. Things changed, though, when a very patient and sensitive social worker convinced Len that respite care may primarily be of benefit to Mrs Baker, without saying anything about the benefits for Len. It was also suggested that during this period of respite Len may wish to attend a carers' support group where he could exchange information and describe to other carers his own experiences of caring. This was not perceived as a threat, particularly because even though the social worker would be present, the group was mainly run by and for the other carers. Indeed, Len would not just be a recipient of help, but a contributor.

It was not long before the process of change began. Respite took place more often and Len became a regular attender of the carers' group. He did not seek anything beyond this. He coped with his own distress in the group and in himself. But people did notice a change in him and the evidence for this came not so much from Len, but from the professionals with whom he had occasional contact. No longer was his house described as the 'dragon's den'. People enjoyed paying a visit.

Support groups: professionally led and self-help

Respite aims to help carers by providing some relief from the task of caring. A different focus is found in support groups, which aim to provide information and advice to participants, as well as a forum for general discussion and the identification of common experiences. The goal, in the longer term, is for participants both to receive advice and information from those who organize the group, but also to help each other by offering their own experience relating to the themes identified. The groups may be structured, meaning they have a clearly articulated aim, process and content, or they may be unstructured.

Broadly speaking, support groups are not the same as therapy groups. The latter are set up with a specific therapeutic agenda and are facilitated by someone with therapeutic training and experience. Participants in a therapy group attend with a clear understanding of its therapeutic aims and make a conscious choice to expose themselves to the therapeutic process. Support groups, though, do not pretend to offer formal therapy.

A structured support group may, for example, aim to provide information to carers in the form of a number of theme-centred meetings. One theme might be 'The Stress of Caring' and the organizer of a group on this theme would aim to present information about stress and its various manifestations with a view to identifying common experiences among the participants. This would provide an opportunity for carers to recognize that they share a number of difficulties and individual carers may then be able to describe their own solutions to the difficulties identified, which could be of use to the other participants. This may then be followed by other themes. For instance, a doctor may talk about the effects of medication, a social worker may describe available social care and benefits, or a clinical psychologist may introduce techniques of stress management and problem-solving. The information provided is educational in the sense of providing information which may not otherwise be accessible and providing carers with an opportunity to ask questions. In addition, something like a 'Stress of Caring' group will often sow the seeds for further exploration by the carer, who may develop an interest in, say, personal counselling to examine further any problems identified in the group.

George Davis is attending a group arranged by the local sexual medicine clinic. The purpose is to provide advice and information to the participants, who are all carers of someone with HIV, and the group is facilitated by one of the clinic nurse specialists. George is talking about his partner, for whom he is the principal carer. The theme for this session is stress management and the topic is 'What Causes Stress?' For George, stress results from having his needs 'ignored' by his partner:

George: I realize now, I thought he didn't care about my feelings, but I'm not sure I ever told him what they were. I've always found it difficult to ask for something for myself. I always want him to know what I want and then I get disappointed so often and that makes me angry.

The nurse was very clear that this was not a therapy group and that it would be inappropriate to spend time in the group focusing on George's specific emotional needs. Nevertheless, he did not want to discount George's comments.

Helper: We can't go into this in detail in this group, but perhaps you need to consider how often this happens. Is it just your partner, or does it happen with others too? Is it just happening now, or has it happened for some time? If you or any of the others want to talk further about the issues you have identified, contact me after the group finishes.

The outcome was that George approached the nurse later and, having considered what he said, recognized a long line of similar disappointments. He decided he needed to understand more about why and how this tendency had developed. 'What can I do?' he asked. The nurse suggested he investigate the possibilities for counselling. He suggested an introductory book on counselling and gave a list of locally accessible counselling organizations.

Problem Solving

When faced with problems, there are essentially two strategies. On the one hand, the individual can behave in ways that create distance between himself or herself and the problem. On the other hand, the individual can face the problem directly. With the former, distancing strategies include avoidance, passivity, denial and the inhibition, suppression or repression of emotions. Sometimes, in the short term, these strategies can be a useful initial response to the problem, creating some space and time to muster resources. In the longer term, however, they can create problems in themselves; and often people seeking help from counsellors and clinical psychologists need help because they have become entrenched in a strategy of avoidance that has outlived any initial usefulness and, instead, has led to a sense of powerlessness and lack of control. At some point, if the problem is to be coped with, a need arises to face up to and resolve it. Problem-solving provides a means to achieve this.

Active attempts to maintain a sense of mastery over a situation are associated with a beneficial outcome for the carer and the person cared for and correspondingly positive attributions. Thus direct action in the form of problem-solving is likely to increase the individual's sense of self-efficacy and self-worth. Problem-solving is a specific approach which can be integrated with the core skills described in Chapter 5. It is a form of stress management and is founded on the principles of cognitive-behavioural psychology. The basic assumption is that problem-solving is appropriate when a carer is having difficulty coping, despite having coped in the past. There should be evidence that the individual possesses the capacity and basic personal resources to cope, but has temporarily lost this capacity as a result of the stresses of dealing with the responsibilities and demands of caring. In other words, the person's normal strengths have been, temporarily, undermined as a result of the difficult adjustments required in becoming, and maintaining the role of, a carer. In my experience this is very characteristic of carers, the majority of whom have coped in the past, but have been temporarily undermined by the stresses of being a carer.

Caplan (1961, cited in Hawton and Kirk, 1989) has defined the circumstances where problem-solving is likely to be helpful when:

a person faces an obstacle to important life-goals that is, for a time, insurmountable through the utilisation of customary methods of problem-solving. A period of disorganisation ensues, a period of upset, during which many abortive attempts at solutions are made.

The goals of problem-solving are defined by Nezu and Perri (1989) as:

- to help individuals identify the reasons for their current incapacity to cope – this involves identifying the life circumstances that have triggered the present difficulties;
- to minimize the impact of the current experience of not coping on future attempts to cope;
- to increase the effectiveness of coping with current problems;
- to provide a foundation of skills that will be used to prevent difficulties arising in the future.

Hawton and Kirk (1989) suggest that the question of whether the problem-solving approach is appropriate for a particular individual depends on:

- whether the problem(s) can be specified clearly in terms agreed between the helper and the person seeking help;
- whether the goals identified by the person seeking help are realistic and achievable;
- there being no severe and acute psychiatric illness in the person seeking help (basically, if the person is suffering from problems in maintaining contact with reality, he or she will not be suitable for this approach);
- there being mutual agreement between the person seeking help and the helper about the aims and limits of problem-solving – it is a practical approach aimed at dealing with present problems and developing skills for dealing with future difficulties.

Problem-solving involves a series of stages first in analysing and then in attempting a solution to identified problems. The stages are:

- Define the problems as clearly as possible. What are the problems?
- Place the problems identified in order of priority. Which is the most important problem? Which one do you want to deal with first (and second and third, etc.)?
- Starting at the top of the list of priorities, generate as many potential solutions as possible (do this in turn for each problem on this list).
- Evaluate the pros and cons for each potential solution.
- Make a choice between the alternatives.
- Put the chosen solution into practice.
- Monitor and evaluate progress and outcome.
- Move on to the next problem in the list.

Define the problems as clearly as possible

The golden rule is *be as specific as possible.* For instance, if the carer says 'I can't cope,' get more detail. Ask, for instance:

- What sort of thing are you finding most difficult at the moment?
- Are you not coping all the time or just sometimes?
- Are there any particular circumstances when it is more difficult to cope than usual?
- What are you doing that is not working as you want it to?
- What do you think you should be doing that you are not?

Jane is the mother of Peter, a 12-year-old boy with learning difficulties. Jane is married to George and their relationship has become increasingly strained both by the demands of their mutual role as carers and also by George's increasing absences from home because of work. The helper, in this case, is the volunteer counsellor from the local carers' centre. Jane has been visiting the centre from time to time to acquire information about local support and resources and, on this occasion, she has asked if there is someone who might be able to help her with her own needs. She feels at the end of her tether.

Jane: I just find it all so impossible. I am really in a mess. I don't know what to do. Sometimes I really feel I can't go on.
Helper: You feel life is that bad?
Jane: Yes.
Helper: Well let us see if we can understand a bit more about what

exactly it is that makes it seem that bad to you. You say that it is all impossible, but I am not sure what all *is. Can you be a bit more specific in describing the problems you are having? Is it every single bit of your life, or just some parts of it?*

Jane: *Oh, it's everything.*

Helper: *Well, tell me about the last time you felt you couldn't deal with a problem. When did that last happen?*

Jane: *Well, this morning was a good example. We had some forms to fill in from the Department of Social Security. I hate forms. I can't do them. I don't have the time. I can't face thinking about it. And then my son Peter was upset because the day centre has organized a trip and it seems it is full, so he can't go, and I had to spend all morning comforting him.*

Helper: *Well, already I can see that there are a number of areas that are difficult for you. Are there any others?*

Jane: *Well yes, there is George; he is my husband. I just don't see him these days. He is always working late. And me, I am just a total mess. Look at me, I am overweight and constantly tired: I just don't have a life.*

Helper: *Okay, so there is the Social Security form, there is the day centre, there is Peter, your son, there is your weight and there is your husband, George. Let us just write those down. Will you do it? (The helper hands Jane a pen and paper and Jane lists the problems identified so far.)*

Helper: *Thank you. Now, is there anything else?*

Jane: *Isn't that enough?*

Helper: *Okay, well it seems to me that there are clearly some difficulties and maybe it all seems overwhelming because you just don't know where to start or how to go about it. Do you think it is possible to put your list in order of importance? Is there any one problem that is more important to you than the others, or that you would like to deal with first?*

Jane: *Well, they all seem important. But I have to have the form returned to the Department of Social Security by the end of the month. It is not so much that I can't do it; I just don't have any energy. Actually, it is not even that. I think the real problem is how unsupported I feel by George. If only he would help more I could deal with the forms and the day centre. Oh, but the more I think about it the more I can see how difficult it is all around. I am such a mess and that is why he spends so much time away at work. I think I have got to sort myself out first. But how am I going to do that?*

Helper: Well, let us just pause for a moment and think about this. You seem to have two sorts of difficulties. One sort is the practical things that you can usually deal with, like the day centre and the form-filling, but you feel you just don't have the energy at present. The other sort of difficulty seems to be about you and your husband. You think he doesn't help enough, but you also think he stays away from home because you feel a mess.

This extract illustrates a common reaction whereby a person may feel overwhelmed not because any single area of difficulty is beyond her or his competence, but because the accumulation of several different difficulties feels overwhelming. In addition, the difficulties taken together can all be related to each other such that the practical difficulties probably have their roots in the relationship difficulties.

The helper's task in this example was to enable the carer to move from a position of feeling overwhelmed by a general sense of not coping to a position of identifying specific areas of difficulty. This in itself can bring a feeling of relief, marking a transition from feeling powerless to cope, to feeling that each difficulty represents a step along the way to restoring the ability to cope.

Place the problems identified in order of priority

The helper summarized the problems that had emerged from the discussion. She next asked Jane to make a list of all the problems that had been identified and any more she might like to add, so that they would all be clearly stated and recorded. She also suggested that Jane should put the list in order of priority, from the most important problem at the top of the list, to the least at the bottom. In doing this, Jane, with the aid of the helper, was able to distinguish two different classes of problem: practical and relationship. The result of this process is that the foundations are now laid for a problem-solving approach.

Generate as many potential solutions as possible for each problem identified

The next step is to think of potential solutions. Fundamental to finding a solution is to identify *how* the identified problem might change. What are the aims of change? What differences does Jane want to make in her life? It is important to be as creative as possible in generating ideas for solutions. A useful technique is 'brainstorming', in which the carer produces a host of possibilities ranging from the sublime to the ridiculous. These can be refined at a later stage. The point is that the carer should be as uninhibited as possible in these initial stages. It is also useful to write this list down. Jane decided that her aim was to repair her relationship with George, if possible, but if not, then at least to put an end to the state of affairs that had developed between her and him. Her unexpurgated list concerning George included the following:

- Shoot George.
- Talk to George.
- Ask George to leave.
- Force George to do more around the home.
- Hire a private detective to investigate whether George is really working late, or if he has some other reason for being home late.
- Contact Relate (the marriage guidance organization) and ask George if he would attend.
- Lose weight (because this would make her feel more attractive and better about herself and also give George more reason to spend time with her).

Evaluate the pros and cons for each potential solution

Having thought of some potential solutions, choices need to be made. Some of the proposals will be viable, others will not. A benefit of the uninhibited list is that it allows the expression of some basic feelings. So, for instance, if 'Shoot George' is written light-heartedly, it nevertheless expresses a basic frustration common in many relationships where there is felt by one partner to be an unequal distribution of responsibilities; and this can provide a basis for further discussion later.

The next task is to consider the pros and cons of each potential viable solution. One useful strategy at this stage is to consider the costs and benefits and to list these. On the left hand side of the page, for example, list what is to be gained. On the right hand side list what, if anything, is to be lost if a particular strategy is tried. It is also worth taking into account any others who might be affected by a choice. Is their role critical to the outcome of the strategy? For example, where does Peter fit into Jane's plans? It would clearly be unwise to make a unilateral decision about a supposed solution that only causes other problems. In this case, it would be necessary to include Peter in the equation.

Make a choice between the alternatives

A choice of strategy needs to be made and the plan put into action. Jane decided that her first strategy should be to try to talk to George. She felt that she could not do this on her own, but needed help, so to begin with she would discuss her options with the helper. She also decided she would like to lose weight and get fitter. This was to enable her to feel good about herself and she decided she would do this whatever the outcome with George. Some of the options Jane felt were unrealistic. For instance, asking George to leave would, at this stage, be premature and would have a profound effect on Peter. If necessary, that might be her last resort.

The point of listing and then choosing between alternatives is that it allows the carer to be as uninhibited and truthful as possible. It may involve expressing the otherwise inexpressible. For instance, a carer might want to register her anger towards the person she cares for. Another may wish to express his frustrations and unrequited desires. There are many constraints within a caring relationship that prevent these feelings being acknowledged even though the individual may be very conscious of them. Expressing them openly can itself bring great relief – 'There, I have said it' – and this can have therapeutic consequences.

Sometimes people fear that if they openly express their inner thoughts and feelings in this way, it may make the present situation untenable and lead to a more serious breakdown of coping. My own view is that even if the thoughts and feelings are presently unexpressed they are nonetheless powerful and they do already, in the present, have an impact on the carer's world. The chances of a breakdown in coping are not any greater because the thoughts and feelings are finally articulated. More often there can be great relief and the person can see that choices have to be made, either to go ahead as things are, or change direction.

Put the chosen solution into practice (time for action!)

Helper: So, what are you going to do?
Jane: I will speak to George. To begin with I am just going to ask him to discuss things with me. I am going to tell him I am unhappy and I want our relationship to improve and also that I need some help with the tasks around the home, like filling in that Social Security form. I know it is not a one-way process and he will have things he wants to say too. If he responds, we can begin to try to work something out together. I am also going to contact Weight Watchers and see about getting healthier.

It might be that Jane would like to go through her plans in detail with the helper before speaking to George, looking for possible difficulties that could arise and rehearsing what to say or do. When the time is right and all the plans have been made and rehearsed, the time will come to act.

Monitor and evaluate progress and outcome

Helper: Well, how did it go?
Jane: It was a disaster. He just did not want to know about talking things through. I really gave him every opportunity. I didn't rush things; I didn't push, but he wasn't interested.
Helper: So, where does that leave you now?
Jane: Well, it is back to the drawing board, I suppose. If George doesn't want to be around, then I can't force him. It is going to take a while to get used to the idea, but I used to manage to live independently before I met George, so there is no real reason why I can't now. But can we talk about this a bit more? I know what my 'head' tells me is probably right, but my 'heart' is not always so rational. I don't want to make any wrong decisions.

Move on to the next problem in the list

Look at each problem in turn. Often, though, once the first problem has been addressed, the other problems begin to sort themselves out or recede in significance. Whatever problems remain, however, can be dealt with in the same way.

Emotion-focused coping leading to problem-solving

This example of problem-solving has focused on the practicalities of decision-making and has illustrated strategies that are useful for people generally when faced with problems. It will be apparent, though, that alongside the practicalities there are also likely to be emotional issues. For instance, Jane has introduced the idea of living independently without George. The reality is that while that might seem like a good idea in principle, there are going to be moments of self-doubt and feelings of uncertainty that also have to be attended to if the practical solution is to have a chance of succeeding.

The task of coping, then, can be *problem-focused* or *emotion-focused*, although these are not mutually exclusive approaches. Problem-focused coping involves trying to change the perceived cause of the problem, using techniques such as those described. Emotion-focused coping involves trying to adapt one's feelings so that the emotional response to the problem is bearable rather than overwhelming. The helper must be prepared to work at both levels: with the emotions as well as the practicalities. This is illustrated in the next case example.

Mrs Mercer was worried about the medical treatment her husband was receiving. Mr Mercer was a retired accountant who suffered a heart attack in the middle of a supermarket. He had received medical treatment but now, some six months later, he was still experiencing chest pains. He was admitted to the coronary care unit at the local hospital. When Mrs Mercer visited him, she was shocked by how poorly he looked and he complained to her that the staff had changed his tablets and this was worrying him.

This also worried Mrs Mercer and the worry had grown to proportions that were affecting her ability to cope. She would anxiously lie awake at nights feeling a failure for being unable to tackle the problem of the tablets directly with the hospital staff. In the daytime she was tired and listless, uncommunicative and withdrawn. She met with the community physiotherapist at her local health centre in order to receive information about the help provided after discharge from the unit where her husband was now receiving treatment. Following the stages described, the helper (the physiotherapist) had engaged Mrs Mercer in a process of identifying, exploring and clarifying her own specific difficulties in dealing with the stresses of being a carer. Now the time had come to clarify the precise questions that were of concern and to set some goals.

Helper: Are there any specific questions you would like to ask the medical staff?
Mrs Mercer: Yes. I want to know why they reduced his medication.

He's obviously not better yet and I can't understand why he needs less medication now. I'm worried they're just giving up on him.
Helper: So you have two questions. One is whether Mr Mercer is getting better or worse at the moment and the other is why they are giving less medication than before?
Mrs Mercer: Yes. Oh, but I get so worried. What if he is getting worse? Part of me doesn't really want to know the answer.
Helper: Yes, I can understand that, but does not knowing really make you feel less worried?
Mrs Mercer: No, I worry about him anyway. It seems I worry whichever way it goes.
Helper: Well, if I understand you correctly, you seem to be saying that finding the answers to your questions isn't necessarily going to make you worry more: you worry anyway.
Mrs Mercer: Yes, I hadn't thought of it that way.

Let us, first of all, consider how to characterize Mrs Mercer's difficulties. We can begin by recognizing her symptoms: worry, insomnia, listlessness, withdrawal and lack of communication. We have discovered some reasons for these symptoms and the consequences are a feeling of failure and self-reproach for not being able to sort out the problem of the tablets. Although the information is not provided directly in the extract, we can hypothesize about the probable chain of reasoning that underlies Mrs Mercer's emotional state. We know, from Chapter 3, that feelings of failure are interpreted by an individual and an explanation is constructed. In Mrs Mercer's case there is self-reproach: she evidently blames herself for what she perceives as her failure. Thus her self-worth is diminished. All of this is affecting her capacity to cope and this, in turn, compounds the sense of failure, triggering the classic spiral that, ultimately, can lead to depression.

In the above extract, Mrs Mercer's attitude had begun to change following the helper's last comment. This provided a different perspective on Mrs Mercer's dilemmas. This is an example of *re-appraisal*, the process of rethinking the meaning and implications of events and providing a new view which gives the opportunity for negative, pessimistic and self-diminishing self-appraisal to become more positive and realistic with correspondingly positive implications for self-worth.

However, despite recognizing that logically there was nothing to prevent her finding out more about her husband's condition,

Mrs Mercer remained apprehensive. Her head, so to speak, told her one thing, but her heart told her another.

Mrs Mercer: I know I should just ask how he is getting on, but I can't. I'm afraid.
Helper: Afraid?
Mrs Mercer: Yes. I am afraid that he may be getting worse. I don't really want to think about that.
Helper: It must be very difficult to think about. I suppose there must always be a possibility that someone might get worse. What do you know about your husband's condition and his chances of recovery?
Mrs Mercer: Very little. I know it is serious, but I don't really know how things will be in the future.
Helper: Would it help, do you think, if you had more information?
Mrs Mercer: Well, I suppose I would know a bit more about whether there is anything to worry about.
Helper: Yes. Look, there is no easy answer to something like this. We have to recognize the fact that neither of us knows how Mr Mercer is getting on at the moment. It is possible that anyone's condition may get worse. Asking questions sometimes gives us answers we don't want to hear.
Mrs Mercer: Yes, that is what I am afraid of.

This extract demonstrates a process of emotion-focused coping. It also illustrates the point that, in reality, the various components of helping such as, in this case, emotion-focused coping and problem-solving can and do overlap. A major anxiety for Mrs Mercer is the possibility of her husband deteriorating. It has been difficult, though, for her to face up to this possibility and many of her fears have been inhibited. If fears are inhibited, they can take on a magnitude that is disproportionate to reality. Now, however, in the above extract, the fears are discussed openly for the first time. In so doing, her fears follow the same principle that applies to anything that is first avoided and then acknowledged. The initial avoidance compounds and magnifies the fears; the subsequent discussion reduces those unnecessary layers of anxiety. The person may still be left with a level of distress, but this is a more authentic level, and ultimately easier to cope with, than the magnified and distorted level that existed before.

It took a further meeting focusing on this theme for Mrs Mercer to discover for herself that her fears could be addressed by removing the uncertainty that surrounded her husband's condition. Of course, she would not then be entirely relieved of concern for her husband's health, but her concern would be based on reality rather than unsubstantiated fear. In the next session Mrs Mercer made the decision that she would like to remove the uncertainty. In doing this she would be addressing directly her distress caused by the unnecessary worry, although she knew that the distress caused by her natural concern would remain. Mrs Mercer's ability to recognize this distinction was crucial in enabling her to act. She was then able to formulate a plan: she would ask about the medication and her husband's prognosis. The next question was practical: how to put her plan into action?

Facilitating action

Helper: How can you find the answers to your questions?
Mrs Mercer: Well, it's so difficult when you see the specialist. I don't want him to think I don't have confidence in him and, anyway, he's always so busy and surrounded by all the other doctors. I feel embarrassed.
Helper: Do you have regular contact with any other staff at the unit?
Mrs Mercer: Yes, there's Janet. She's the sister. She's lovely. Maybe I could ask her.
Helper: Good idea. Now you need to decide when you will ask and what you will ask. You've already decided who you will ask. Let's deal now with when.
Mrs Mercer: Yes. I'm due to go up there tomorrow. I'll phone beforehand and make sure Janet is on duty and that she will have time to talk to me.
Helper: Excellent. Now, what exactly do you want to ask? It might help to write the questions down so that you don't forget anything. Does that feel all right?
Mrs Mercer: Yes. I'll do that tonight, after dinner. I'll just have to find a quiet half hour then: this is important.
Helper: Okay, then that's agreed. Let's hope you will find the answers to your questions. But if not, at least you will be clearer about what the problems are and we can look for ways of working on them.

As a result of this help, Mrs Mercer was able to speak to Janet and ask her the questions. In fact, it was not the ordeal she had originally anticipated. The fact that she had an opportunity to express her fears and worries to the helper beforehand had itself brought much relief. She had been enabled to bring her worst fears to the fore and, in the cold light of day, they were not overwhelming. This experience enabled her to change her perception of things so that she became a problem-solver and this gave her a sense of control over her problems. By the time Mrs Mercer saw Janet, she was much more realistic and less anxious. Janet explained her husband's condition and the reasons for the changes in his medication. Mrs Mercer was reassured to learn that her husband's treatment was still progressing and that there was no sense of the staff giving up on him. Her fears and anxieties were dispelled. She remained naturally concerned for her husband, but her concern now was realistic and in proportion to the circumstances.

Emotional Help: Complex Issues

The advice provided to the reader so far in this book is based on the view that you as a helper will wish to extend and develop your skills in order to improve the help you are able to give to carers. This raises an important question. How far can you go with your own helping skills and at what point should you consider referring on to a specialist in counselling or psychological therapy? In some cases the carer can be enabled to be specific about the nature of his or her difficulties and, as the examples demonstrate, there is a logic in the strategy that can be developed to address the problems identified. In other cases the logic of the situation may be obscured by psychological processes which are unclear but have to do with competing demands or pressures on the carer, either from within himself or herself or from other people. An understanding of these issues will enable the helper to consider the boundaries of his or her skills and the question of when specialist help from a clinical psychologist or qualified counsellor may be indicated.

One of the greatest problems in coping in general is avoidance. Avoidance usually indicates a degree of uncertainty in the carer about the best course of action. Sometimes avoidance is a conscious strategy and sometimes it is an unconscious manifestation of underlying doubt, uncertainty or ambivalence.

While avoidance can, in the short term, be beneficial, allowing the person time to adapt and get used to the implications of change, in the longer term it is likely to lead to an exacerbation of the problem and feelings of failure. Failure to cope at this level is characterized by physical avoidance of the situation or persons who elicit the fear, as well as the denial of feelings associated with the problematical situation. A number of categories of avoidance may be distinguished.

Avoidance as emotional denial

People report a variety of emotional reactions to traumatic stress, the most typical of which are some combination of anger, shock, fear, anxiety, guilt and hopelessness. The first thing to say is that these are all natural and normal emotional responses, in the short term. Problems arise when the normal response becomes extended in time and unresolved, or when it is in some way difficult or seems impossible to express the natural feelings. In many societies and cultures, this is a reflection of social sanctions on the direct expression of these emotions. It is difficult to make an absolute statement about this because of the variability in cultural attitudes and conventions (see, for example, Zborowski, 1952, on cultural differences in the expression of emotion). However, even taking into account this inter-cultural variability, there remain limits on the direct expression of manifest emotion, and there is a common view that the unrestrained expression of emotion is tantamount to the loss of control.

In circumstances, therefore, where the expression of emotion is problematical there may be a denial of feelings. This denial can take various forms, and I will say more about the different types of denial later in the chapter. As a generalization, however, the denial of feelings is associated with not coping and the task of helping is to identify the process of denial and, gently and gradually, to enable the individual to feel safe enough to begin to acknowledge these unexpressed feelings. For instance, many carers feel anger towards the person for whom they care. This is a difficult emotion to acknowledge because it contradicts a central assumption of caring, which is that caring is an altruistic task. However, if anger is born of frustration, and frustration is inevitable in caring, then anger is much more widespread than many carers would acknowledge. The consequences of not acknowledging anger are found in feelings such as guilt, where the carer is conscious but ashamed of the anger; indirect hostility, which can often be an unconscious manifestation of denied anger; direct hostility, where anger is associated with blame; and detachment, where thoughts and feelings are isolated from each other and the feelings become inaccessible. Similar processes can occur with other emotions, such as fear, or hopelessness. The emotions, because they are denied, become distorted and this can lead to the gradual erosion of the relationship between those involved, with adverse psychological consequences all around.

Avoidance as passivity

If a person fears something then the *anticipation* of the aversive experience can lead to avoidance. Avoidance brings relief from fear and anxiety and so the avoidance becomes intrinsically rewarding. If a behaviour is rewarding, it is more likely to be repeated and thus patterns of behaviour become established. It will be apparent that this sequence of events can lead to a vicious circle of avoidance, which reinforces the idea in the individual's mind that the event being avoided really is to be feared. In this way the individual never puts his or her expectations to the test. Aversiveness is assumed rather than experienced directly. Furthermore, as avoidance becomes established so the possibility of direct action decreases. In time the person ceases to respond, and becomes withdrawn and passive.

Avoidance as 'distorted' thinking

Avoidance is often accompanied by a tendency towards questionable patterns of thinking in which the beliefs a person expresses are not always consistent with the evidence. The anticipated negative outcome is magnified in the person's mind and becomes the only conceivable reality, to the exclusion of all other alternatives. Thus the person distorts reality to fit in with his or her conceptions and begins to rationalize and justify the avoidance: 'Oh, I didn't want to go there anyway'; 'I wouldn't do it if they paid me'; 'It is for the best'.

Avoidance and the self

The consequences of avoidance behaviour in general permeate through to the self as a sense of failure. The individual is aware, consciously or unconsciously, of a discrepancy between what *ought* to be done and what *is* done. Condition 1 for the preservation of self-worth is undermined (see Chapter 3). The meaning of the behaviour is evaluated and a self-critical attribution is made. Consequently, the complex emotions of guilt and self-blame are likely to ensue from avoidance strategies, leading to loss of confidence and reduced self-worth.

To tell or not to tell?

The following case example examines the issue of avoidance in relation to a frequently occurring dilemma faced by helpers and carers. The question is, who should be told what, and when? This is not just a question for helpers; it is often also a reflection of dilemmas experienced by the carer. Sometimes carers and the person for whom they care may have, or believe they have, different informational needs. There may, indeed, be conflict between the expressed needs of each person involved. Such discrepancies need to be identified and clarified when they occur. If the differences provide the basis for actual or potential conflict between carer and person cared for, then it may be necessary to consider specialist help from a clinical psychologist or formally qualified counsellor for one, both, or all the individuals concerned.

I have referred earlier in the book to the need to provide information and to the fact that this can pre-empt future emotional difficulties by relieving uncertainties and anxieties. In some instances, the fact that there is a need for specialist counselling or psychological therapy at some stage may reflect a lack of attention to the individual's informational and emotional needs at an earlier stage, leading to an exacerbation of emotional distress in the present. That is why it is so important for helpers to ensure where possible that these fundamental needs are met as early as practicable. At other times the need for specialist counselling or psychological therapy may reflect individual difficulties based on past experience of dealing (or failing to deal) with stress and trauma, or there may be long-standing characteristics of the relationship between carer and person cared for which complicate the carer's response to the other's present needs.

John and Hendra are the parents of Marty, a six-year-old girl who was about to go into hospital for investigation of a suspected disease. Marty appeared to be unconcerned, although her behaviour had changed recently. In particular, she had been very reluctant to go to school. Her parents were naturally anxious about Marty going into hospital. Even though they knew the investigations were necessary, they were afraid in case something more serious should be discovered. John and Hendra felt at a loss over how to deal with the situation. Should they play it down, put it to one side and not discuss it with Marty? Or should they talk to her about it? And what about their own feelings of distress? Should they hide these from Marty: put on a brave face? How would Marty react if she knew about her parents' distress?

They decided to talk to a helper (perhaps their doctor, or a nurse at the children's hospital, or some other health professional, or a teacher at Marty's school) about these dilemmas. In this case the helper, their doctor, decided she had the skills, as described in this book, to meet John and Hendra's needs. At this stage, at least, specialist help did not seem to be indicated.

The doctor first of all allowed John and Hendra time to express their concerns and identify their dilemmas. She then enabled John and Hendra to formulate a practical, problem-solving strategy, which was to spend an evening making a list of all the pros and cons for either discussing things fully with Marty or not doing so. She also suggested a preliminary visit by John and Hendra to the children's ward at the hospital, where they could talk to the staff in more detail about the procedures involved and ask advice about what information is usually provided to children at this stage. These suggestions were helpful because they enabled John and Hendra to shift from feeling they had an insurmountable problem to recognizing that there were avenues they could explore and that they themselves could become problem-solvers.

Nevertheless, and despite this, it was also evident that John remained ambivalent about talking to Marty. John's non-verbal behaviour showed that he was not content. He frowned; he sat hunched and anxious; he looked unhappy. The doctor was able to recognize this and reflect back to John the discontented message he seemed to be conveying.

Helper: I am not sure you are convinced, John, that talking to Marty may be the right thing to do?
John: I just can't see how she will cope.

The task now for the helper was to attempt to understand John's doubts and examine whether they were valid in the circumstances. The problem was that they may not have been and if they were not then the reasons for not talking to Marty were unsound. The helper, then, had to examine the underlying reasons for John's doubts and apparent avoidance of the issues. Where there was evidence of questionable patterns of thinking it would be necessary to identify and challenge the underlying reasons and then explore alternative possibilities. The focus, of course, is on the *carer's* beliefs rather than his or her assumptions about the beliefs of the person for whom he or she cares. The *underlying beliefs* must be made explicit and then challenged by reference to evidence.

When discussing this with John, it became apparent to the helper that part of his reasons for protecting Marty was the fact that John himself could not stand to see her upset.

Helper: What will happen if she gets upset, John?
John: If she gets upset she will cry and feel awful and I just can't stand to see her like that.

It thus became apparent in the discussion that there were certain assumptions being made by John which were debatable. In essence, John held a belief that can be expressed as follows: 'If I talk to Marty about the illness she will become upset. If she becomes upset she will be unable to cope. If I avoid talking about it, she will remain calm. Avoiding the topic is best for her.'

The problems in this pattern of thinking can be seen first of all in the supposed, but unnecessary, link between becoming upset and being unable to cope and secondly in the proposed reason for avoiding talking. An underlying assumption in the example is that people cannot tolerate painful feelings and once exposed to such feelings they do not recover. This is, in fact, a common belief encountered in these circumstances. The helper, using the relationship skill of advanced empathy, gently pointed out that in protecting Marty, John was also protecting himself and that this too may be part of the reason for his ambivalence.

Helper: John, I know you are concerned for Marty's feelings and that you want what is best for her, but it seems as though there may be something more. What about your feelings? How does it make you feel?
John: Wretched.

If this can be done in a considerate and non-threatening way, the individual can begin to discover something of the motives behind his or her behaviour. In questioning these, he or she can then decide if the strategy that had been chosen is really the best available. The questions that might arise in such a case are: What is it that underlies the person's self-protective stance? What are the self-concepts that accompany such an attitude? It might be that there are underlying beliefs concerning the other's illness that indicate self-criticism, or diminished self-worth. Talking about the illness might bring these negative self-concepts to the fore, and so it is avoided. The individual's task is to understand the relationship between his or her avoidant behaviour and self-concept. If the basis for any feelings of powerlessness can be put into perspective and seen not as personal failure, but as an inevitable consequence of difficult circumstances, then the effects on the individual may be less distressing and less disruptive.

In this example, John's motive for not discussing the topic was seen to be ambiguous. Initially, the motive was presented as being protective of the other, which was partly true, but not the whole reason. Later it became apparent that self-protection may also have been involved. Self-protection in these circumstances is not the same as selfish protection. Parents looking after vulnerable children often experience a sense of personal powerlessness, and acknowledging this can be very demoralizing. Protecting themselves from the full impact of that powerlessness is quite natural and understandable. However, there are circumstances when it can also become problematical, as in this case.

It is difficult to say whether the help that was provided to John and Hendra, up to this point, was sufficient for their present needs. One possible outcome was that John would use his new insight into his dilemmas as a basis for resolving his ambivalence and working out his own solution, in conjunction with Hendra, to Marty's current needs. I would suggest that in terms of non-specialist helping, this was as far as the helper could reasonably go. If, on the other hand, John has long-standing difficulties of which his current dilemma is just one instance, then he may need longer-term and more specialist help. The helper, therefore, must make a choice based on his or her knowledge and estimation of John and his general coping abilities. The helper could, of course, ask John if he feels the need for further help in this matter. If, after this, the helper remains unsure, it would be appropriate to contact a specialist, such as a clinical psychologist, and, with John's approval, discuss the case and seek advice about what the next step may be. John, of course, would be a participant in any decisions that were made about his needs.

Ignorance is bliss?

A similar issue arises in the next case example. In this case, however, the helper judged that specialist help was definitely indicated and, with the carer's consent, a referral to a counsellor was made.

Janet was the daughter of William and Margaret. William had a life-threatening kidney disorder. Janet was suffering stress symptoms that were interfering with her work and leading to excessive sick leave which was jeopardizing her employment. On a visit to the hospital, she mentioned this to one of the nurses she felt she could trust.

Janet's own view was that the stress was a direct consequence of her worries over her father's illness. She felt she should be coping in order to support her parents through this troubled time, but it was becoming harder and harder. These difficulties led to feelings of failure and guilt. The nurse (the helper) decided that it would be beneficial for Janet as well as her parents if Janet had an opportunity to talk in some detail about her difficulties. The discussion began by examining the effects of William's illness on all the family.

Helper: It must be very difficult for you all to cope at the moment?
Janet: Oh no, my parents aren't having any problems at all. They just get on with things.
Helper: What do you think it is that enables them to cope so well?
Janet: Well my mother just won't have it that my father is seriously ill, and of course he doesn't realize how serious it is.
Helper: You think he doesn't know how ill he is?
Janet: No, we haven't told him. At least we can spare him that.

This illustrates a common belief, within both families and the medical professions, that it is in the patient's interests, sometimes, to remain ignorant. Is it in the patient's interests? Why? When? How do we know? I have had this discussion with numerous professional colleagues and there really is a split in opinion. I have also heard the view that, in effect, 'ignorance is bliss' from a number of carers. Obviously, generalizations are impossible and unhelpful. It is unreasonable to insist that an individual always should or always should not be told the truth about a serious illness. I will refer later to some research that suggests people who use denial with certain kinds of illness may have a better prognosis than people who accept their illness. Nevertheless, what does seem to be common, in my experience, is that often the 'blissfully ignorant' patient is no such thing. Often he or she has a suspicion, or a fear, of the seriousness of the condition. Often the lack of certainty is far from blissful. So the very basis of a belief such as Janet's may be unfounded.

Janet's case was complex and the helper made a decision that she had neither the time, the facilities, nor the experience to provide all the help Janet needed with her particular stress, which had become incapacitating, and the more general issues of how to deal with her father's illness. With Janet's permission, she contacted a counsellor attached to the local clinical psychology department and asked if he would take the referral, which he agreed to do.

The following interchange occurred after Janet and the counsellor had agreed to meet regularly to examine further Janet's difficulties. This was their second meeting.

Counsellor: You feel you have to protect your father from the knowledge that he is seriously ill?
Janet: Yes, of course. He's unhappy enough about being ill, why make him even more unhappy?
Counsellor: How can you be sure it would make him more unhappy?
Janet (in disbelief): Well of course it would. Would you like it if someone told you that you were seriously ill?
Counsellor: Well, I have known people who were relieved to be told the full details of their illness. What really made them unhappy was the uncertainty and the feeling of having things kept from them.
Janet: I can't believe that. How could anyone cope with that?

In the above extract the opportunity has been created for Janet to consider points of view other than her own. If other people can sometimes cope with full knowledge of the seriousness of their illness then the certainty with which she and Margaret have decided to keep William ignorant may need to be reconsidered. She may learn that apparent ignorance is often only a mask. Perhaps William does have suspicions. If he does, perhaps these create fears, fantasies and anxieties which are worse than being told the truth. In addition, if William's condition is life-threatening, perhaps he would regret not having time to prepare for his death. There may be things he would want to say to his family and friends before he dies. Perhaps there are material arrangements he would like to make, such as ensuring his will is in order, his accounts are settled, his family is provided for and so forth.

As it turned out, the main reason for Janet and Margaret's strategy was more to do with Margaret's inability to face the truth than with William's inability to hear it. By ostensibly protecting William, Margaret too was spared the anguish of his illness, at least temporarily: the anguish was only deferred. And Janet's stress symptoms were one sign of the price paid for this avoidance. Let us now consider how the session with Janet developed.

Counsellor: I wonder why you feel so strongly that no one could cope with knowing they are seriously ill?
Janet: Oh I don't know. It's so complicated. We've always been funny about any kind of illness. You just don't talk about it in my family. If anyone is ill you ignore it. I remember when I was about six, I fell and broke a bone in my hand. It was a week before I told my mother and she just told me to stop fussing. The teacher at school made my parents take me to the doctor.
Counsellor: How do you feel about that now?
Janet: I'm appalled. What a ridiculous way for my mother to act.

At this point the reasons behind the decision not to tell William about his condition are beginning to be explored. As the session went on Janet was able to acknowledge that what she initially expressed as *her* feelings about her father's reactions were, in fact, simply the expression of a deeply entrenched family 'culture' concerning illness. Janet was able to re-examine whether this culture was really one to which she wished to subscribe. Was it just habit or was it her preferred choice? She was able to reconsider whether to continue in the same way or, instead, to begin to question this attitude towards illness.

The next question was whether and how to challenge her mother's assumptions about William's capacity to cope. In the end Janet decided her parents' views were too ingrained and that she could not and should not challenge them at this late stage in her father's life. The important difference for Janet, however, was that instead of feeling forced into this position by the habits of her family's culture, she was now able to feel in control of the decision, making it on her own rather than someone else's terms. It was this change in perspective that made the difference between not coping as she had been and being in control and thus coping subsequently.

On the basis of this information we can now understand Janet's initial stressed state as a symptom of conflict resulting from the discrepancy between her parents' expectations of how illness should be responded to – with denial – and Janet's own previously inhibited disapproval of this attitude. This engendered the complex emotions of shame, guilt and hopelessness due to a perceived failure to cope adequately as defined by her mother's attitude to coping and this eroded Janet's sense of self-worth. Her initial way of coping was to subscribe to her parents' denial by inhibiting her own feelings on the matter, thus maintaining a precarious hold on the approval of her parents. Later, though, as a result of counselling, she was able to identify and resolve the conflict this induced and then, independently of her parents' injunctions, make her own decision about whether or not to continue to inhibit those feelings.

Denial and coping: a caveat

Although denial is often associated with not coping, there may be exceptions. I mentioned earlier the difficulty in generalizing about the adaptiveness or otherwise of some coping strategies. Denial is a case in point. There is evidence that *some* people who use denial as a coping mechanism may have a better prognosis than those who give emotional expression to their feelings about being ill (Dean and Surtees, 1989; Levenson *et al.*, 1989; Greer, 1979). This is an important point for helpers to consider: it may *not* always be appropriate to 'break down' defences. On the other hand, some of the disengagement strategies *may* be unhelpful and the scope for enabling the development of more adaptive strategies remains an important aim in helping. The only rule here is to treat each case individually.

My own view is that denial is not a single entity: there are different forms of emotional denial. *Suppression* can be viewed as a *consciously adopted* and freely chosen form of denial that should be distinguished from *repression*, which is associated with non-conscious processes, and *inhibition*, where the conscious choice goes against the individual's better instincts. If a person *chooses*, albeit tacitly, to suppress his or her feelings, then this choice should be respected. Repression and inhibition, by contrast, carry the implication of no choice. Rather the person seems forced by little-understood fears to follow a particular course of action. In this case an examination of the underlying fears and assumptions may, in the right circumstances, be appropriate and, ultimately, allow the individual a greater freedom of choice. Janet began by inhibiting her feelings, and thus going against her better instincts, which caused her distress. She ended, though, by choosing to suppress her feelings, which marked the change from being out of control of her decision to being in control of it.

Denial as healthy defence

The final example of a complex issue which may require specialist help illustrates the distinctions between the different forms of denial by focusing on the case of denial as emotional suppression. This example is of a young couple, one of whom was diagnosed as having cancer. Their dilemma was how to balance being positive and maintaining hope with acknowledging the reality of the disease and its ultimate effects.

'It's odd,' she said, 'although part of me knew he was dying, I could never really admit it.' Mary had cared for her husband Paul during his cancer and up to his death at the age of 35. One of Paul's favourite sayings had been 'While there's life, there's hope.'

This saying encapsulates a major theme and a major dilemma faced by many of those who care for someone who is seriously ill. The dilemma is: what is the boundary between hope and denial? Is entertaining the possibility of remission compatible with acknowledging the possibility of death?

The solution to the dilemma is to be found at a very subtle level of human communication. Modern cognitive psychology and brain science has begun to explain differences between 'knowing with the head' and 'knowing with the heart' (LeDoux, 1998; Teasdale and Barnard, 1993). Many helpers will be familiar with the carer's view, expressed in various ways, which states: 'I know what you are saying is true, but I don't believe it.' That is to say: 'My head tells me one thing, but my heart another.' This same distinction between heart and head is to be found implicitly within the communications of carers faced with such dilemmas as described.

When I first encountered this phenomenon, my assumption was that each individual should be able to acknowledge and articulate the possibility of death. He or she may also wish to keep hope alive, but not at the cost of denying death. And so I looked for signs of the capacity consciously to acknowledge what I saw as the reality of eventual death. Rarely, though, was such acknowledgement forthcoming. More often only the hope was articulated and I was left with a discomfort over the wish to challenge, but the need also to allow the individuals to maintain some adaptive defences. In the end I often felt that I was colluding in the denial.

Later, though, I began to see that my expectations had been unrealistic insofar as the acknowledgement of death is sometimes present but is not always stated explicitly. A far more subtle level is involved at which the dilemma *is* communicated, but indirectly. The following is an extract of a session involving Paul and Mary. They too wanted to keep hope alive. I felt that part of my job was to balance their hope with the other possibility, that Paul would die soon. His treatment had reached its end and the growth remained untouched, with a high probability of having spread. I had seen Paul and Mary over a period of weeks during medical treatment and now the current medical treatment was complete.

Psychologist: So, the treatment is finished, but the growth is still there?
Paul: Well I was hoping the growth would have reduced, but at least it hasn't grown. I don't know. We just have to keep on being positive. I've heard of people recovering from this and I'd like to be one of them.
Psychologist: Mary, how do you feel about this?
Mary: Yes, we just have to hope it will get better. He looks so well and I think he's doing as much as anyone could to fight this.
Psychologist (to both): Is it difficult to have to keep fighting all the time?
Paul: I can't see there's any alternative.

During the rest of the session Paul and Mary repeatedly confirmed their 'positive' attitude and declined the opportunity to articulate other possibilities such as fear, doubt or uncertainty.

In the next session the same theme was pursued (now listen to the 'heart' speaking).

Paul: I've been thinking. I was reading an article about 'quality of life'. I just hope they don't think that by stopping my treatment now they're doing it to improve my quality of life. I know they do make those decisions. They say: 'Well we could keep him going for another couple of months but it would take so much out of him he would be better off without further treatment.' Well I hope they're not thinking that about me. I want to be the one who makes that decision. I'm the best judge about my quality of life, not them. If I have the chance to live a couple of months extra then I want to be the one to decide.

Mary: We want to decide, Paul, both of us.

Paul: Yes, I know Mary, both of us.

The difference between this excerpt and the earlier one is that in the earlier session the possibility of death had been suppressed. In the terms I have already described, this was a form of adaptive denial which allowed Paul and Mary to maintain a balance of hope alongside the reality of Paul's illness. In the later session Paul and Mary began to shift the balance to allow a little more of the reality to seep into their discussion. There was still a degree of suppression, but it was not so much as earlier. Both were now allowing the possibility of death to be discussed. It was still not explicit, but was clearly alluded to by Paul when he talked about quality of life and living a couple of months extra. It was important that Paul and Mary were allowed to proceed at their own pace. They were not avoiding the reality, but were gradually negotiating their own path through the difficult issues they both faced and this enabled them both to cope.

Whether to refer on

These, then, are some examples of the more complex issues that can arise in helping. Of course, there are many more and these examples are just a small sample of the variety of difficulties and dilemmas faced by carers, patients and helpers. It is important, though, that the reader should not infer from the examples that someone like Janet or Paul and Mary can *only* be helped by a professional counsellor or psychological therapist. There *is* a decision to be made by all helpers about how far their own skills extend and there is a danger that must be avoided in helpers overextending themselves. Nevertheless, for all of these reservations, it is important not to lose sight of the fact that there remains much that can be done within the competence of a sensitive helper who builds upon the basic helping skills he or she uses daily.

In considering whether to refer on, the helper should take account of:

- the extent of the carer's present difficulties – whether they are specific to a clearly identifiable problem, or reflect a longer-standing difficulty in dealing (or failing to deal) with any form of stress and trauma;
- whether there are long-standing problems within the relationship between carer and person cared for which complicate the carer's response to the other's present needs;
- whether the helper has the time, facilities, or experience to provide all the help the carer needs.

In addition, there are some problems for which specialist help is clearly indicated. For instance, if a carer has specific symptoms such as obsessive-compulsive behaviour, or suffers panic attacks, or is so severely depressed as to be entirely uncommunicative, he or she is likely to need the help of the local mental health services. If the carer has become dependent on alcohol, there may be local voluntary or statutory organizations which specialize in such problems. If the stress of caring for a sick or disabled parent or child has created strain in a marital relationship, the local marriage guidance service may be the appropriate organization to help. If a carer suffers a bereavement, there are organizations that specialize in providing support for the recently bereaved.

If any of these conditions obtain, or if there is any doubt in your mind about whether help is feasible in a particular case, then the best advice is to consult with an experienced clinical psychologist or qualified counsellor. Clinical psychology services will generally be prepared to discuss these issues with helpers and will welcome your enquiry. They may also be prepared to offer you specific supervision for certain complex cases, so that you are able to continue the work yourself under the guidance and support of the supervisor.

Concluding Remarks

This chapter has illustrated the application of the previously described basic helping skills to some of the difficulties experienced by carers. It is suggested that it is possible to offer help in ways that can either boost or undermine the carer's morale and it is important that help is offered in a way that *affirms* the carer's efforts and is perceived by the carer as supportive.

Examples are given of three overlapping strategies for helping in terms of information and advice, support and emotional help and problem-solving. It is noted that all the different forms of help can and do overlap in particular cases. The whole is greater than the sum of its parts, and the whole will take account of all levels of the carer's difficulties, ranging from the practical to the emotional. Reference is also made to a number of complex issues which raise the question of when to seek specialist help from a qualified clinical psychologist or counsellor.

Summary

❑ Information and advice are often required on practical matters such as financial support, mobility aids, voluntary or statutory organizations which may be able to provide further help.

❑ Information also provides empowerment and is a means of laying the foundations for emotional help.

❑ Material and emotional support may take various forms, such as:

- increased contact with others in order to decrease social isolation (e.g. membership of carers' organizations and support groups);
- respite, for both the carer and the person cared for.

❑ Emotional help also involves enabling individuals to acknowledge and talk honestly about their emotions in relation to the illness or disability of the person cared for and its effect on themselves and others. This may provide some relief in itself, but is often a prelude to problem-solving.

❑ Problem-solving refers to the development of skills that will enable the carer or, in some cases, the person cared for, to identify

continued

continued — — — — — — — — — — — — — — — — —

and then deal more effectively with a specific problem or range of problems. The steps in problem-solving are:

- define the problems as clearly as possible;
- place the problems identified in order of priority;
- starting at the top of the list of priorities, generate as many potential solutions as possible;
- evaluate the pros and cons for each potential solution;
- make a choice between the alternatives;
- put the chosen solution into practice;
- monitor and evaluate progress and outcome;
- move on to the next problem in the list.

❑ Complex psychological issues may arise in working with carers and the helper is encouraged to consider when referral on for specialist help may be required.

❑ As a general rule, specialist help or advice should be considered if:

- there is evidence in the carer of a long-standing difficulty in dealing (or failing to deal) with any or most forms of stress and trauma;
- if there are long-standing problems within the relationship between carer and person cared for which complicate the carer's response to the other's present needs;
- if the helper has insufficient time, facilities, or experience to provide all the help the carer needs.

❑ In addition, specialist services are available for mental health problems, alcohol misuse, marital difficulties and bereavement.

❑ Clinical psychology and counselling services will generally be prepared to arrange consultation and supervision for helpers to advise on referral on, or to support the helper with a complex case.

❑ In the event of referring on for specialist help, however, the carer is always consulted and is a participant in any decisions regarding the referral.

7

Conclusions

The aim of this book has been to provide a description and understanding of the experience of caring and to illustrate ways in which we all, as helpers, can facilitate the process of enabling carers to cope more satisfactorily with their difficult task. Any description, though, however vivid, is an understatement of the reality of caring. Only direct experience can bring us close to understanding just what it is like to be a carer. For all the limitations, however, it is hoped that the information included in the previous chapters will be of use both to helpers of all kinds and, through them, to carers.

Issues for the Helper

Any book that claims to provide guidelines to readers about how best to do some task – in this case to be an effective helper – must also acknowledge the variability among *helpers*. There is variability in skill, experience and opportunities to provide effective help. The best advice for all helpers must be first of all to recognize your limits, but do not underestimate your potential. Above all, though, do not begin something you cannot finish and if you encounter difficulty, seek help yourself.

Although the skills described in this book are designed to enhance and complement your routine care in whatever professional role you undertake, there is no doubt that they can be further enhanced if you are able to undertake some kind of extended training in these skills. Counselling is an increasingly widespread practice and there are a variety of organizations that specialize in training in counselling skills. This ranges from short-term introductory courses in local educational establishments to lengthy nationally organized training courses. One of the main benefits of training is the contact you will have with other trainees. If you can become involved in a network of helpers who are all concerned with improving their helping skills, then this will provide considerable impetus to support your own efforts: the best form of skills development comes from the feedback you receive from others.

In addition, whatever help you are able to provide, you need to ensure that you know where *you* can get help when you need it with the difficulties intrinsic to the helping role. Professional counsellors and psychological therapists are expected to have regular clinical supervision. Any helper may expect to be exposed to some of the same stresses and difficulties experienced by those counsellors or psychological therapists. Although the extent of these stresses and difficulties *may* be relatively less, reflecting the focus of your particular work, it is nonetheless important to be aware of the potential need yourself for supervision.

Supervision may take the form of meetings with peers or colleagues involved in similar roles, or with managers (although supervision of this kind must be kept separate from other forms of management), or even formal supervision from a counsellor or psychological therapist, if the nature of your work warrants it. The need for supervision is not a reflection of relative inexperience or lack of competence; even the most experienced workers continue to require supervision throughout their professional lives. Supervision protects the helper from becoming over-involved, or from making basic errors, such as taking responsibility for the carer rather than acting as a facilitator, or overextending his or her role in some other way. More and more organizations are recognizing the need for regular supervision for all staff whose work brings them into a regular helping role.

The idea of supervision also raises the important issue of referral on, to which I have already alluded in Chapter 6. As with any skill, helping has its limits. Bearing in mind the diversity of the carer's needs, it is likely that some of these needs will require forms of help that you are unable to provide (this will be true at some time for all helpers). It is important for you as a helper to know where specialist help can be found. There are likely to be a number of voluntary and professional specialist organizations established nationally and locally. If you have a nearby carers' centre or carers' bureau, they will provide you with all the information you need about local resources available for carers. Local advice bureaux will have relevant information about a range of statutory and non-statutory services and organizations. The local library too may have an information section with directories of qualified and registered clinical psychologists, other psychological therapists and counsellors. In brief, be aware of networks within and outside your organization: when and where and how to get help for your patient or client and yourself and how to refer on for specialist or more in-depth work.

Helping also takes time and resources. The common complaint of many health and social services professionals is that there is too little time for all the demands their work entails. The combination of large client caseloads and organizational bureaucracy can mean that the professional helper feels unable to meet all the demands made and, regrettably, it is often patient or client care that is compromised. If you as a helper wish to improve the quality of help you provide, in this case to carers, then to some degree you may find yourself swimming against the tide of all your professional responsibilities. There is a problem when the demands made outweigh the resources available and the literature is replete with accounts of professional burnout as a result. The symptoms of burnout in Table 2 apply equally to helpers and carers and you will do well to be familiar with the signs and symptoms in yourself. In a similar way, the strategies described in this book for helping carers cope can be applied to you, the helper. Use the problem-solving skills yourself when you encounter a difficulty. Recognize the importance of support for yourself and identify sources of support within the work environment. Recognize too that you may occasionally need respite from the demands of being a helper.

Another resource implication may arise if helping carers is perceived by others in your organization to be an extension or development of your normal role. You may find, for instance, that your manager or your professional colleagues will be concerned if you are seen to spend time with someone other than the primary recipient of your service. I regret to say that I know of one organization in which staff were explicitly told that carers' needs were outside the remit of the staff's role and therefore staff were discouraged from spending too much time with relatives. I am not suggesting that this is typical, but it will always be helpful if you can gain agreement from the administration and management of the organization in which you work that helping carers is part of your remit. This avoids ambiguity in times of uncertainty. In addition, an explicit recognition of the legitimacy and relevance of the helping activities described in this book also serves as a precedent for the provision of support for you, the helper, in the form of training and supervision.

Does It Work?

Finally, in these days of increasing interest in the 'evidence base' of various kinds of treatment and intervention, it is appropriate to ask: 'Does it work?' There is evidence that helping skills properly applied in medical settings can confer a number of benefits. For example, it has been shown that the use of counselling and helping skills can improve patients' satisfaction with health care and promote psychological adaptation, which enhances recovery and physical adaptation (Davis and Rushton, 1991). Mullen *et al.* (1997) reviewed 74 studies of patient education in terms of information, advice and basic counselling. They found demonstrable benefit in preventing unhealthy behaviours, such as smoking and alcohol misuse, as well as promoting healthy behaviours, such as exercise and stress reduction. In addition, and importantly, the use of counselling and helping skills have been shown to increase the morale of *staff using the skills* (Davis and Fallowfield, 1991).

Despite these benefits, however, there remains a general question of whether or not the specific techniques of counselling and helping are more effective than standard clinical treatment (e.g. Moynihan *et al.*, 1998; Harvey *et al.*, 1998). However, even in those studies that find standard treatment to be equally beneficial, it is likely that the standard treatment, where it works, does so precisely because the clinician is able to use effective communication skills as part of that treatment (see Chapter 5 of this book on the relevance of relationship skills in general medical procedures). Clearly, further research is necessary before any firm conclusions can be drawn. It does seem increasingly apparent, though, that effective communication is intrinsic to effective helping and the skills described in this book are designed to promote and enhance effective communication.

Does it work for carers?

A number of studies have attempted to evaluate the benefits of helping carers specifically. The usual criterion for defining a helpful intervention is a reduction in carer distress leading to an enhanced ability in the carer to cope, although Brodarty and Peters (1991) also used measures of increased survival rates at home in the persons cared for. Some studies report success in reducing carer distress (e.g. Brodarty and Peters, 1991; Sutcliffe and Larner, 1988). However, other studies report either no effect or mixed results (e.g. Joice *et al.*, 1990; Zarit *et al.*, 1987).

One problem in drawing unambiguous conclusions from such studies lies in the variability of carers' needs, which follows from the variability of carers' problems, described throughout this book. The assumption has often been made that carers will share common needs and thus benefit from common solutions. However, some studies have begun to discriminate the differing needs of carers within a particular population. For example, Bledin *et al.* (1990) were able to distinguish different degrees of hostility and criticism within a group of 25 female carers of a parent with dementia. The distinction between high levels and low levels of hostility and criticism corresponded to differences in distress reported by these carers, so that the former were more and the latter less distressed. In a similar vein, Oldridge and Hughes (1992) distinguish the differing stresses associated with carers of long-term sufferers of schizophrenia compared with carers of recent-onset sufferers. They also make the important point that many in their sample of carers coped without any psychological ill effects. The fact that the sample as a whole comprised carers of people diagnosed as schizophrenic does not mean they all experienced difficulties and in cases where difficulties were experienced they were not necessarily equivalent for all carers.

This highlights the difficulty in making generalizations about the effectiveness of helping skills. The fact is that each carer is different and there are an infinite number of combinations of difficulties that constitute the 'problem' for any particular carer. In order, therefore, to assess the benefits of helping, we need to consider a number of areas of potential help. In the case of carers, the benefits may be defined in various ways. For instance, there may be a reduction in levels of distress experienced in the process of caring, either for the carer or person cared for. There may be a range of new problem-solving skills developed by the carer to facilitate coping and pre-empt further problems. There may also be improvements in the general sense of wellbeing and quality of life of the carer or person cared for, or a reduced utilization of health resources (less medication, fewer visits to the doctor). It will be clear that the question 'Does it work?' demands a full picture of all these potential areas of change and improvement.

However, there may also be some dilemmas. We must also ask for whom the benefits are assumed to occur. To return to an earlier example, is it a successful outcome if the carer's distress is reduced by, say, organizing respite care, while the person cared for becomes more distressed because of the unfamiliar environment, and vice versa? These are difficult judgements to make and each case must be considered individually.

Concluding Remarks

In conclusion, the answer to the question 'Does it work?' is that, in general, the skills described in this book are capable of bringing about valued change. Good communication is fundamental to all helping. Clearly, if someone lacks information and you are able to provide it, your intervention has been helpful, by definition. However, carers often have specific needs and helping skills must be applied to the particular circumstances of each individual. Emotional help and problem-solving are more difficult to evaluate because of the complexity of individual experience. In order to assess the value of these forms of help, we need to learn how to target the help more effectively, to those whose need is greatest. We need to know more about which individuals have difficulty in coping in what situations. We need to know what factors protect some carers from psychological ill effects so that they cope without external help while others experience difficulties. We need to know more about the relationship and the balance between helping carers, on the one hand, and helping those cared for, on the other.

The main point to take away from the examples discussed in this book is that the efficacy of any form of practical and emotional help must be judged in relation first of all to the nature of the problems in a particular case and secondly to the individual's needs derived from difficulties in dealing with those specific problems. The evidence for each individual is in the outcome for that individual, and in the extent to which success achieved as a result of the help you are able to provide can be generalized outside the specific helping context. The question you as a helper must always ask is: *Who* requires *what* help *when*? The skills described in this book will aid you in answering those questions by enhancing your ability to establish a helping relationship, to facilitate communication, to listen and identify the specific needs of individuals and to offer the beginnings of practical and emotional support and problem-solving.

Helping is complex and demanding, but ultimately a rewarding activity, for the helper, the carer and the person cared for. I have tried to provide a positive picture of the potential for helping skills, properly applied. I have also pointed to some difficulties and complexities. However, do not let the caveats and complexities deter you from the main aim of the book, which is to encourage you to develop your own skills and experience. As a professional, you undoubtedly face the complexities of helping in the course of your work and, as I said at the outset, if you come into contact with carers in your professional capacity you already use a variety of helping skills. Some of these may be implicit and undeveloped, but they provide a foundation for the success of your endeavour. You can build on this foundation and improve your skills. In improving your own skills you will be enhancing your role as a helper and the satisfaction you get from your work and you will also be making a contribution to the better care of others. I wish you success in that enterprise.

Summary

❑ There are a number of issues the *helper* must consider in order to maximize the helping skills described in this book.

❑ There is variability among helpers in skill, experience and opportunities to provide effective help and helpers must recognize their own limits as well as their potential.

❑ Helpers may wish to consider gaining extended training in helping skills, which will allow feedback from other helpers with similar interests.

❑ It is important that helpers know where *they* can get help, support and supervision.

❑ Supervision protects the helper from becoming over-involved, or from making basic errors.

❑ Helpers are encouraged to be aware of networks within and outside their organization: when and where and how to get help for their patient or client and themselves and how to refer on for specialist or more in-depth work.

❑ There are a number of practical difficulties, such as too little time for all the demands their work entails and a lack of agreement from the administration and management of the organization about whether helping carers is part of their remit. Agreement needs to be reached between the helper and others in the organization about these issues.

❑ Helping can be stressful and helpers too need to guard against burnout. The strategies described in this book for helping carers cope can also be applied to helpers.

❑ The question is raised of how we assess the benefits of helping and relevant evidence is reviewed which shows a generally positive effect. The evidence of benefit for each individual is to be found in the outcome for that individual and in the extent to which success achieved as a result of the help you are able to provide can be generalized outside the specific helping context.

❑ Helpers must always ask: *Who* requires *what* help *when*?

Appendix A:
Useful Organizations/Agencies – UK

AGE CONCERN (England)
Astral House
1268 London Road
London SW16 4ER
Tel: 0181 679 8000
Web site: http://www.ace.org.uk

AGE CONCERN (Northern Ireland)
3 Lower Crescent
Belfast BT7 1NR
Tel: 01232 245 729

AGE CONCERN (Cymru)
4th Floor
1 Cathedral Road
Cardiff CF1 9SD
Tel: 01222 371 566

AGE CONCERN (Scotland)
113 Rose Street
Edinburgh EH2 3DT
Tel: 0131 220 3345

AL-ANON
61 Great Dover Street
London SE1 4YF
Tel: 0171 403 0888
Web site: http://www.al-anon.org/
Help for relatives of people with an alcohol problem.

ALZHEIMER'S DISEASE SOCIETY
Gordon House
10 Greencoat Place
London SW1P 1PH
Tel: 0171 306 0606
Web site: http://www.alzheimers.org.uk.

ARTHRITIS CARE
18 Stephenson Way
London NW1 2HD
Tel: 0171 916 1500
Web site: http://www.arthritiscare.org/

See also **ARTHRITIS NEWS** (http://www.vois.org.uk/arthritiscare/html/WATS1.HTM), the magazine of Arthritis Care.

ASSOCIATION FOR SPEECH IMPAIRED CHILDREN
121–123 Charterhouse Street
London EC1M 6AA
Tel: 0171 608 1661

ASSOCIATION OF CROSSROADS CARE ATTENDANT SCHEMES
10 Regent Place
Rugby
Warwickshire CV21 2PN
Tel: 01788 573 653

BREAK (Holidays and Respite Care)
20 Hookshill Road
Sherringham
Norfolk NR26 8NL
Tel: 01263 823 170

BRITISH RED CROSS
9 Grosvenor Crescent
London SW1X 7EJ
Tel: 0171 235 5454
Web site: http://www.redcross.org.uk

CALIBRE
(Cassette Library for Blind or Handicapped Children and Adults)
New Road
Western Turville
Aylesbury
Bucks HP22 5XQ
Tel: 01296 432 339/81211

CANCER LINK
11–21 Northdown Street
London N1 9BN
Tel: 0171 833 2818
Fax: 0171 833 4963
Freephone cancer information helpline: 0800 132905
Web site: http://www.easynet.co.uk/aware/contacts/clink/index.htm
Support and information for people with cancer and their carers

CAREMATCH
286 Camden Road
London N7 9JN
Tel: 0171 833 2451
A computer service to help find residential care for physically disabled people.

CARERS' NATIONAL ASSOCIATION
20–25 Glasshouse Yard
London EC1A 4JS
Tel: 0171 490 8818
Fax: 0171 490 8824
Helpline: 0171 490 8898
Web site: http://www.carersuk.demon.co.uk

CARING COSTS
Tel: 0171 250 0370
Campaigning for a better deal for carers.

CONTACT A FAMILY
(Family Groups for Children with Special Needs)
170 Tottenham Court Road
London
Tel: 0171 383 3555

COUNCIL AND CARE FOR THE ELDERLY
Twyman House
16 Bonny Street
London
NW1 9PG
Tel: 0171 485 1566

CRUSE BEREAVEMENT CARE
126 Sheen Road
Richmond
Surrey TW9 1UR
Tel: 0181 940 4818
Counselling advice on practical issues and opportunities for social contact for anyone who has become bereaved.

DIAL UK
Park Lodge
St Catherine's Hospital
Tickhill
Doncaster DN4 8QN
Tel: 01302 310123
Web site: http://members.aol.com/dialuk/dept/dialnet.htm
Disablement information and advice line.

DISABILITY NET
Web site: http://www.disabilitynet.co.uk/
A range of useful resources, addresses and web links.

DISABLED LIVING FOUNDATION
380–384 Harrow Road
London W9 2HU
Tel: 0171 289 6111
Web site: http://www.atlas.co.uk/dlf
An information service for people with disabilities. Also an exhibition
of equipment for viewing only.

DOWN'S SYNDROME ASSOCIATION
155 Mitcham Road
London SW17 9PG
Tel: 0181 682 4001
Fax: 0181 682 4012
Web site: http://www.downs-syndrome.org.uk

HEADWAY (National Head Injuries Association)
200 Mansfield Road
Nottingham NG1 3HX
Tel: 01602 622 382
Provides advice and help.

HOLIDAY CARE SERVICE
2 Old Bank Chambers
Station Road
Horley
Surrey RA6 9HW
Tel: 01293 774 535
Advice on holidays, holiday helpers and travel arrangements.

JOHN GROOMS ASSOCIATION FOR DISABLED PEOPLE
10 Gloucester Drive
Finsbury Park
London N4 2LP
Tel: 0181 802 7272

MENCAP
(Royal Society for Mentally Handicapped Children and Adults)
123 Golden Lane
London EC1Y 0RT
Tel: 0171 454 0454
Web site: http://www.mencap.org.uk

MIND (National Association for Mental Health)
Granta House
15–19 Broadway
Stratford
London E15 4BQ
Information line Tel: 0181 522 1728
Web site: http://www.mind.org.uk

MOTOR NEURONE DISEASE ASSOCIATION
PO Box 246
Northampton
Northamptonshire NN1 2PR
Tel: 01604 250505
Fax: 01604 624726
Helpline Tel: 01345 626 2620
Web site: http://www.businessconnections.com/mnd

MULTIPLE SCLEROSIS SOCIETY
25 Effie Road
London SW6
Tel: 0171 736 6267
Web site: http://www.mssociety.org.uk

See also **JOOLY'S JOINT** (http://www.mswebpals.org), a support
network and Webpal service for people who live with multiple sclerosis.

NATIONAL AIDS HELPLINE
Tel: 01800 567123 (24 hours)

NATIONAL SCHIZOPHRENIA FELLOWSHIP
London Advisory Centre
197 Kings Road
London WC1X 9BZ
Tel: 0171 837 6436

NATIONAL TOILET KEY SCHEME – RADAR
Issues special keys to fit toilets for disabled people. The keys can be
used nationally. To obtain a key write or phone:

RADAR
25 Mortimer Street
London W1N 8AB
Tel: 0171 637 5400

There is a charge for the keys.

PARKINSON'S DISEASE SOCIETY
22 Upper Woburn Place
London WC1H 0RA
Tel: 0171 383 3513

RADAR – The Royal Association for Disability and Rehabilitation
12 City Forum
250 City Road
London EC1V 8AF
Tel: 0171 250 32222
Produces informative publications and monthly newsletters.

STROKE ASSOCIATION
CHSA House
123–127 Whitecross Street
London EC1Y 8JJ
Tel: 0171 566 3000
Web site: http://www.stroke.org.uk/
The Stroke Association works for the prevention of stroke illnesses and to provide sympathetic help for those who suffer and their families.

TERENCE HIGGINS TRUST
52 Grays Inn Road
London WC1X 8JU
Tel: 0171 831 0330
Web site: http://www.tht.org.uk/
Advice and support, and where to go for local information for people with AIDS or HIV and their friends and relatives.

Appendix B:
Useful Organizations/Agencies – US

AL-ANON FAMILY GROUP HEADQUARTERS, INC.
1600 Corporate Landing Parkway
Virginia Beach, Virginia 23454-5617
Tel: (800) 344-2666, (757) 563-1600
Fax: (757) 563-1655
Web site: http://www.al-anon.org

ALZHEIMER'S ASSOCIATION
919 North Michigan Avenue, Suite 1000
Chicago, Illinois 60611-1676
Tel: (800) 272-3900, (312) 335-8700 and (312) 335-8882 (TTY)
Fax: (312) 335-1110
Web site: http://www.alz.org

AMERICAN CANCER SOCIETY (AMS)
Tel: (800) 227-2345
Web site: http://www.cancer.org

AMERICAN SOCIETY ON AGING (ASA)
883 Market Street, Suite 511
San Francisco, California 94103
Tel: (415) 974-9600
Fax: (415) 974-0300
Email: info@asa.asaging.org
Web site: http://www.asaging.org

ARTHRITIS FOUNDATION
1330 West Peachtree Street
Atlanta, Georgia 30309
Tel: (800) 283-7800, (404) 872-7100
Web site: http://www.arthritis.org

CANDLELIGHTERS CHILDHOOD CANCER FOUNDATION
7910 Woodmont Avenue, Suite 460
Bethseda, MD 20814
Tel: (301) 654-8401 or (800) 366-2223
Fax: (301) 718-2686

CDC NATIONAL AIDS CLEARINGHOUSE & HOTLINE
Centres for Disease Control
Post Office Box 6003
Rockville, MD 20849-6003
Tel: (800) 458-5231 (English & Spanish)
TTY/TDD: (800) 2437012
Weekdays 9 a.m. – 7 p.m.

THE COMPASSIONATE FRIENDS
Post Office Box 3696
Oak Brook, IL 60522-3696
Tel: (630) 990-0010
Fax: (630) 990-0246

NATIONAL ALLIANCE FOR RESEARCH ON SCHIZO-PHRENIA AND DEPRESSION
60 Cutter Mill Road, Suite 404
Great Neck, New York 11021
Tel: (516) 829-0091
Fax: (516) 487-6930
Web site: http://www.mhsource.com/narsad.html

NATIONAL INFORMATION CENTER FOR CHILDREN AND YOUTH WITH DISABILITIES (NICHCY)
Post Office Box 1492
Washington, DC 20013
Voice/TDD: (800) 695-0285
Tel: (202) 844-8200
Fax: (202) 884-8200
Web site: http://www.nichcy.org/

NATIONAL INSTITUTE ON AGING (NIA)
Information Centre
Post Office Box 8057
Gaithersburg, Maryland 20898-8057
Tel: (800) 222-2225, (800) 222-4225 (TTY) between 8:30 a.m. and 5:00 p.m. EST
Fax: (301) 478-3014
Email: niainfo@access.digex.net
Web site: http://www.nih.gov/nia/health/health.htm

NATIONAL MULTIPLE SCLEROSIS SOCIETY
733 Third Avenue
New York, NY 10017
Tel: (800) FIGHT-MS or (800) 344-4867
Email: info@nmss.org
Web site: http://www.nmss.org

NATIONAL ORGANIZATION FOR RARE DISORDERS, INC. (NORD)
100 Route 37
Post Office Box 8923
New Fairfield, CT 06812-8923
Tel: (800) 999 NORD or (203) 2746 6518
Fax: (203) 746 6481

NATIONAL PARKINSON FOUNDATION, INC. (NPF)
1501 Northwest 9th Avenue/Bob Hope Road
Miami, Florida 33136
Tel: (800) 327-4545, (305) 547-6666
Fax: (305) 243-4403
Email: mailbox@npf.med.miami.edu
Web site: http://www.parkinson.org

NATIONAL STROKE ASSOCIATION
96 Inverness Drive East, Suite I
Englewood, Colorado 80112-5112
Tel: (303) 649-9299
Stroke Information and Resource Centre: (800) STROKES (787-6537)
Fax: (303) 649-1328
Web site: http://www.stroke.org

References

Abramson, L.Y., Seligman, M.E.P. and Teasdale, J.D. (1978) Learned helplessness in humans: critique and reformulation. *Journal of Abnormal Psychology*, 87, 49–74.

Bandura, A. (1977) Self-efficacy: toward a unifying theory of behavioural change. *Psychological Review*, 84, 191–215.

Barusch, A.S. and Spaid, W.M. (1989) Gender differences in caregiving: Why do wives report a greater burden? *Gerontologist*, 29, 667–676.

Beck, A.T. (1976) *Cognitive Therapy and the Emotional Disorders*. New York: Penguin.

Benson, H. and McCallie, D.P. (1979) Angina pectoris and the placebo effect. *New England Journal of Medicine*, 300, 1424–1429.

Bledin, K.D., MacCarthy, B., Kuipers, L. and Woods, R.T. (1990) Daughters of people with dementia: Expressed emotion, strain and coping. *British Journal of Psychiatry*, 157, 221–227.

Brewin, C.R. (1988) *Cognitive Foundations of Clinical Psychology*. London: LEA.

Brodaty, H. and Hadzi-Pavlovic, D. (1990) Psychosocial effects on carers of living with persons with dementia. *Australian and New Zealand Journal of Psychiatry*, 24, 351–361.

Brodaty, H. and Peters, K.E. (1991) Cost effectiveness of a training program for dementia carers. *International Psychogeriatrics*, 3,11–22.

Coen, R.F., Swanwick, G.R., O'Boyle, C.A. and Coakley, D. (1997) Behaviour disturbance and other predictors of carer burden in Alzheimer's disease. *International Journal of Geriatric Psychiatry*, 12, 331–336.

Compton, S.A., Flanagan, P. and Gregg, W. (1997) Elder abuse in people with dementia in Northern Ireland: prevalence and predictors in cases referred to a psychiatry of old age service. *International Journal of Geriatric Psychiatry*, 12, 632–635.

Davis, H. and Fallowfield, L. (1991) *Counselling and Communication in Health Care*. Chichester: John Wiley.

Davis, H. and Rushton, R. (1991) Counselling and supporting parents of children with developmental delay: a research evaluation. *Journal of Mental Deficiency Research*, 35, 89–113.

Dean, C. and Surtees, P.G. (1989) Do psychological factors predict survival in breast cancer? *Journal of Psychosomatic Research*, 33, 561–569.

Department of Health (1993) *Health of the Nation Key Area Handbook: Mental Illness*. London: HMSO.

Egan, G. (1990) *The Skilled Helper: A Systematic Approach to Effective Helping*. Pacific Grove, CA: Brooks/Cole.

Frankl, V.E. (1959) *Man's Search for Meaning*. New York: Beacon Press.

Freund, J., Krupp, G., Goodenough, D. and Preston, L.W. (1971) The doctor–patient relationship and drug effect. *Clinical Pharmacology and Therapeutics*, *13*, 172–180.

Gibbons, J.S., Horn, S.H. and Powell, J.M. (1984) Schizophrenic patients and their families. A survey in a psychiatric service based on a DGH unit. *British Journal of Psychiatry*, *144*, 70–77.

Gilhooly, M.L. (1984) The impact of care-giving on care-givers: factors associated with the psychological well-being of people supporting a dementing relative in the community. *British Journal of Medical Psychology*, *57*, 35–44.

Gilleard, C.J., Gilleard, E., Gledhill, K. and Whittick, J. E. (1984a) Caring for the elderly infirm at home: a survey of the supporters. *Journal of Epidemiology and Community Health*, *38*, 319–325.

Gilleard, C.J., Gilleard, E. and Whittick, J.E. (1984b) Impact of psychogeriatric day hospital care on the patient's family. *British Journal of Psychiatry*, *145*, 487–492.

Good, B.J. and Good, M.J.D. (1982) Toward a meaning-centred analysis of popular illness categories. In A.J. Marsella and G.M. White (Eds) *Cultural Conceptions of Mental Health and Therapy*. Dordrecht: Dreidel.

Grad, J. and Sainsbury, P. (1965) An evaluation of the effects of caring for the aged at home. In *Psychiatric Disorders in the Aged*. Manchester: World Psychiatric Association.

Green, H. (1988) *Informal Carers*. London: HMSO.

Graham, C., Ballard, C. and Sham, P. (1997) Carers' knowledge of dementia, their coping strategies and morbidity. *International Journal of Geriatric Psychiatry*, *12*, 931–936.

Greer, S., Morris, T. and Pettingale, K.W. (1979) Psychological response to breast cancer: effect on outcome. *Lancet*, *ii*, 785–787.

Guntrip, H. (1971) *Psychoanalytic Theory, Therapy and the Self*. London: Hogarth Press.

Hall, J.N. (1990) Towards a psychology of caring. *British Journal of Clinical Psychology*, *29*, 129–144.

Harvey, I., Nelson, S.J., Lyons, R.A., Unwin, C., Monaghan, S. and Peters, T.J. (1998) A randomised controlled trial and economic evaluation of counselling in primary care. *British Journal of General Practice*, *48*, 1043–1048.

Hawton, K. and Kirk, J. (1989) Problem-solving. In K. Hawton, P.M. Salkovskis, J. Kirk and D.M. Clark (Eds) *Cognitive Behaviour Therapy for Psychiatric Problems: A Practical Guide*. Oxford: Oxford University Press.

Hogbin, B. and Fallowfield, L. (1989) Getting it taped: the bad news consultation with cancer patients. *British Journal of Hospital Medicine*, *41*, 330–333.

Horvath, A.O., Gaston, L. and Luborsky, L. (1993) The therapeutic alliance and its measures. In N.E. Miller, L. Luborsky, J.P. Barber and J.P. Docherty (Eds) *Psychotherapy Treatment Research: A Handbook for Clinical Practice*. New York: Basic Books.

Irwin, M., Brown, M., Patterson, T., Hauger, R., Mascovic, A. and Grant, I. (1991) Neuropeptide Y and natural killer cell activity: findings in depression and Alzheimer caregiver stress. *FASEB Journal*, 5, 3100–3107.

Joice, A., Thomson, M. and Glynn, A. (1990) Carers support groups: meeting the needs of carers and staff. *British Journal of Occupational Therapy*, 53, 136–138.

Kiercolt-Glaser, J.K., Dura, J.R., Speicher, C.E., Trask, O.J. and Glaser, R. (1991) Spousal caregivers of dementia victims: longitudinal changes in immunity and health. *Psychosomatic Medicine*, 53, 345–362.

Knussen, C. and Cunningham, C.C. (1988) Stress, disability and handicap. In S. Fisher and J. Reason (Eds) *Handbook of Life Stress, Cognition and Health*. Chichester: John Wiley.

Krause, I.B. (1989) Sinking heart: a Punjabi communication of distress. *Social Science and Medicine*, 29, 563–575.

Lazarus, R.S., Kanner, A.D. and Folkman, S. (1980) Emotions: a cognitive phenomenological analysis. In R. Plutchik and H. Kellerman (Eds) *Emotion: Theory, Research and Experience* (Vol. 1). New York: Academic Press.

LeDoux, J. (1998) *The Emotional Brain*. London: Weidenfeld and Nicolson.

Levenson, J.L., Mishra, A., Hamer, R.M. and Hastillo, A. (1989) Denial and medical outcome in unstable angina. *Psychosomatic Medicine*, 51, 27–35.

Levin, E., Sinclair, I. and Gorbach, P. (1989) *Family Services and Confusion in Old Age*. Aldershot: Gower Publishers.

Littlefield, A., Lieberman, L. and Reynolds, L.T. (1982) Redefining race: the potential demise of a concept in physical anthropology. *Current Anthropology*, 23, 641–655.

Luborsky, L., Crits-Christoph, P., Mintz, J. and Auerbach, A. (1988) *Who Will Benefit from Psychotherapy? Predicting Therapeutic Outcomes*. New York: Basic Books.

Matson, N. (1994) Coping, caring and stress: a study of stroke carers and carers of older confused people. *British Journal of Clinical Psychology*, 33, 333–344.

McCalman, J.A. (1990) *The Forgotten People: Carers in Three Minority Ethnic Communities in Southwark*. London: King's Fund Centre.

McCann, K. (1991) The work of a specialist AIDS home support team: the views and experience of patients using the service. *Journal of Advanced Nursing*, 16, 832–836.

Menzies-Lyth, I. (1988) *Containing Anxiety in Institutions: Selected Essays*. London: Free Association Books.

Morris, R.G., Woods, R.T., Davies, K.S. and Morris, L.W. (1991) Gender differences in carers of dementia sufferers. *British Journal of Psychiatry, 158* (Suppl. 10), 69–74.

Moynihan, C., Bliss, J.M., Davidson, J., Burchell, L. and Horwich, A. (1998) Evaluation of adjuvant psychological therapy in patients with testicular cancer: a randomised controlled trial. *British Medical Journal, 316,* 429–435.

Mullen, P.D., Simons Morton, D.G. and Ramirez, G. (1997) A meta-analysis of trials evaluating patient education and counseling for three groups of preventive health behaviors. *Patient Education and Counseling, 32,* 157–173.

Nezu, A.M. and Perri, A.G. (1989) Social problem-solving therapy for unipolar depression: an initial dismantling investigation. *Journal of Consulting and Clinical Psychology, 57,* 408–413.

Noon, J.M. (1992) Counselling GPs: the scope and limitations of the medical role in counselling. *Journal of the Royal Society of Medicine, 85,* 126–128.

Noon, J.M. (1998) From placebo to credebo: the missing link in the healing process. *Pain Reviews*, in press.

Noon, J.M. and Lewis, J.R. (1992) Therapeutic strategies and outcomes: perspectives from different cultures. *British Journal of Medical Psychology, 65,* 107–117.

Oatley, K. and Bolton, W. (1985) A social-cognitive theory of depression in reaction to life events. *Psychological Review, 92,* 372–388.

Oldridge, M.L. and Hughes, I.C. (1992) Psychological wellbeing in families with a member suffering from schizophrenia: an investigation into longstanding problems. *British Journal of Psychiatry, 161,* 249–251.

Pomara, N., Deptula, D., Galloway, M.P., Lewitt, P.A. and Stanley, M. (1989) CSF GABA in caregiver spouses of Alzheimer's patients. *American Journal of Psychiatry, 146,* 787–788.

Rogers, C.R. (1961) *On Becoming a Person*. Boston: Houghton Mifflin.

Roth, A. and Fonagy, P. (1996) *What Works for Whom? A Critical Review of Psychotherapy Research*. New York: Guilford Press.

Rowlands, O. (1998) *Informal Carers*. London: HMSO.

Scottish Schizophrenia Research Group (1985) First episode schizophrenia (IV): psychiatric and social impact on the family. *British Journal of Psychiatry, 150,* 340–344.

Steptoe, A. (1991) The links between stress and illness. *Journal of Psychosomatic Research, 35,* 633–644.

Strong, S.R. (1968) Counseling: an interpersonal influence process. *Journal of Counseling Psychology, 15,* 215–224.

Sutcliffe, C. and Larner, S. (1988) Counselling the carers of the elderly at home: a preliminary study. *British Journal of Clinical Psychology*, 27, 177–178.

Teasdale, J.D. and Barnard, P.J. (1993) *Affect, Cognition and Change*. Cambridge: Cambridge University Press.

Thomas, D.R. (1986) Culture and ethnicity: maintaining the distinction. *Australian Journal of Psychology*, 39, 371–380.

Triandis, H.C. (1989) The self and social behaviour in differing cultural contexts. *Psychological Review*, 96, 506–520.

Twigg, J. (Ed.) (1992) *Carers: Research and Practice*. London: HMSO.

Twigg, J. and Atkin, K. (1993) *Carers Perceived: Policy and Practice in Informal Care*. Buckingham: Open University Press.

Weiner, B. (1985) An attributional theory of achievement, motivation and emotion. *Psychological Review*, 92, 548–573.

Wing, J.K. (1981) From institutional to community care. *Psychiatric Quarterly*, 53, 139–152.

Wu, D.Y.H. (1982) Psychotherapy and emotion in traditional Chinese medicine. In A.J. Marsella and G.M. White (Eds) *Cultural Conceptions of Mental Health and Therapy*. Dordrecht: Dreidel.

Zarit, S.H., Anthony, C.R. and Boutselis, M. (1987) Interventions with care givers of dementia patients: comparison of two approaches. *Psychology of Aging*, 2, 225–232.

Zborowski, M. (1952) Cultural components in response to pain. *Journal of Social Issues*, 8, 16–30.

Index